COOKING, BLOKES + ARTICHOKES

BRENDAN COLLINS is executive chef of Birch, Larry's, and The Corner Door in Los Angeles. He has appeared on Spike TV's *Bar Rescue* and MTV's *House of Food*, as well as The Esquire Channel's *Knife Fight*. He currently lives in Los Angeles with Eden, his wife, and Saffron, his daughter.

Drawing on his training in butchery and belief in using the whole animal, Collins is dedicated to using only the best ingredients and cooking food that he likes to eat. He worked at several prominent restaurants in London, including those of Marco Pierre White, before moving to L.A. He combines impeccable French technique, seasonal California ingredients, and his inimitable "British lad" attitude to his cuisine.

COOKING, BLOKES + ARTICHOKES

A MODERN MAN'S KITCHEN HANDBOOK

BRENDAN COLLINS

FOREWORD BY CURTIS STONE
PHOTOGRAPHY BY JEAN CAZALS

KYLE BOOKS

CONTENTS

BRENDAN COLLINS: NO BULLSHIT BLOKE, NO BULLSHIT FOOD.

Bren and I met over 15 years ago whilst working the stoves at Marco Pierre White's revered restaurant Quo Vadis in Soho, London. We worked alongside each other for only a couple of years, however it was here that skill, technique, work ethic, and a solid culinary foundation were drummed into us 17-hour day after 17-hour day— and here that the bromance was born.

Even if I wanted to, I can't seem to escape this bloke. Interestingly, we've both wound up as expat chefs navigating the restaurant scene in Los Angeles. Brendan gained more freedom to explore and define his personal cooking style here, and has earned immeasurable success and respect in our adopted city. While I bloody enjoy a feed at the restaurants he currently helms, Birch and Butcher's Dog, I'm lucky enough to be a frequent face in his home, too. And that means I'm on the receiving end of his simple and hyper-seasonal "California ingredients meets impeccable French technique meets British lad" home-cooked food. Yum!

There's no doubting that my mate knows his way around an animal and ensures everything from a pig's head to a lamb's belly tastes utterly succulent and addictive. Pulitzer Prize-winning food writer for the *LA Times*, Jonathan Gold, says Collins "is at heart a big meat guy," which is absolutely fair game, however don't be skipping over his vinaigrettes, pickles and condiments, "Veggies" and "Pudding" chapters (for those not wised up on Brit speak, pudding is a term for all desserts).

Every recipe has rallied for its place on these pages. I know because I've been there on the family and friends nights, tasting his restaurant plates prior to the doors officially opening and it was no different with his first book. (By the way, first book! Awesome achievement mate!!!) Someone had to make sure his brioche doughnuts packed just the right balance of butter, bourbon, and sweetness, and that the potatoes cooked three-ways were equally delicious when mashed, boiled, or turned into triple-cooked chips—those chips are devilishly good stuff! I'm an absolute sucker for paella. I love Spanish food and have spent quite a bit of time there—Bren's Quinoa and Shellfish Paella takes me right back to the shores of Valencia, the birthplace of paella, whilst simultaneously reminding me that his 10+ year tenure in Southern California has had its way with him, too.

Beyond his Brit-lad, pub loving, "meat man" exterior, Brendan is really a big softie and is forever encouraging of his mates in the industry. I love that in this book, he gets a chance to share his knowledge, experiences, and passion with a bigger audience now (to you, ya smart cookies who have bought this book!) and he'll no doubt inspire you to cook anything from a classic Lemon Tart to a Duck and Walnut Terrine. I'd go as far as to say, this is one of those extra special cookbooks you want to read and cook your way through from cover to cover. Do this and I know you'll gain newfound confidence and competence in the kitchen and you'll add some truly impressive dishes to your repertoire. Plus (and this is the best bit), you'll be eating some downright delicious food and bringing plenty of happiness to the special people in your life.

Bren, you're a cheeky bastard mate, but I love ya! Wishing you all the success in the world with *Cooking, Blokes + Artichokes*. It's a winner.

CHEERS ALL,
Curtis

INTRODUCTION

MY VIEWS ON FOOD ARE QUITE SIMPLE: it should be fresh, tasty, and no more complicated than it needs to be. That isn't some kind of "ethos" dreamed up over days spent gazing philosophically at a bunch of radishes. It's the only thing that makes sense to a bloke raised above pubs in the north of England.

When I was young, my parents worked as pub relief managers; when the owners went away on vacation, my folks would step in, take over shop, and run the business temporarily. Moving through England from pub to pub, I learned a lot about life and something about cooking. There's no real equivalent to England's country pubs in the United States. In little towns and along rural byways all across the nation, they function as coffee shop, bed and breakfast, and restaurant—not to mention post office, town hall, senior center, confessional, and communal living room.

The way that some kids love to take apart stereos or build model airplanes, I always gravitated to the kitchens with their hissing pans and warm smells.

This was before anybody used the word *gastropub*, when the food you found in rural pubs was pretty much universally unaffected, homely fare. But there was good cooking and bad cooking, and even at the age of ten I knew the difference between the two. Some pubs ran Sizzler-style operations, slinging freezer-burned burger patties and canned vegetables, just a notch above fast food. Others took a real interest in local ingredients and from-scratch preparations. I remember one kitchen helmed by a legit old cruise liner chef making his own jus and hollandaise sauce, serving local game meats and whatever fresh vegetables he could get his hands on, in some middle-of-nowhere village. That was, and still is, my idea of how good food ought to be.

After my parents split up, I went to live with my grandparents, and it was there that I had my first true education in eating with the seasons. My granddad approached food with the thrift and self-sufficiency of a man who lived through the war and, worse, postwar rationing. He had his greenhouse and a little orchard at the top of the garden, and from that we had tomatoes, cucumbers, and zucchini in summertime, apples, pears, carrots, and turnips in winter. He raised pigeons and chickens, and we ate them too.

Becoming a chef was quite a natural transition. At the age of fifteen, I left school, left home, and never looked back. I enrolled in cooking school; I got my degree on a Thursday and by Sunday was on a train to London looking for work. I was seventeen. That was the beginning of a restaurant career that has taken me through the kitchens at Le Gavroche, Quo Vadis, Mélisse—some of the best and swankiest restaurants in London and Los Angeles. I've cooked some pretty fancy food over the years, but the country cooking of my boyhood has always remained at the front of my mind. I've never lost sight of what a good, honest homemade dinner looks like.

I find that food has gotten too complicated for my tastes these days. Restaurant dishes tend toward the experimental, heady, and, frankly, weird. Dinner has turned into an opportunity for a chef to test the bounds of his own creativity and invention, and the ingredients sometimes feel more like a dare than a proper meal: dehydrated scallop chips, fermented grasshopper paste, foraged lichen. If you ask me, it's a distraction from the real purpose of a restaurant, which is to feed people well. Leave them full and happy. And more than ever, the way we chefs cook in restaurants influences the way people cook at home.

Flip through today's food magazines and cookbooks and what you find is restaurant food—dishes designed to be cooked inside the confines of a professional kitchen that don't make a whole lot of sense in the home. Restaurant kitchens, with their battalions of hot-footed cooks, dedicated dishwashing staff, walk-in refrigerators, industrial venting systems, high-end ingredient suppliers, and hundreds of paying customers, are set up for cooking food with lots of pieces and steps. Home kitchens, built to feed families, are not. If I spent my days off trying to cook the food that I make at Birch in my home kitchen—that pokey little room with a couple square feet of counter space and burners that barely get hot, by restaurant standards—I'd have nothing but headaches. Home cooking and restaurant cooking are simply two different beasts, and a cookbook made up of restaurant dishes only discourages anybody picking up a knife to learn.

This is not a book about my restaurant, Birch. It's not a commentary on contemporary Los Angeles dining, or an ode to British gastropubs, or a food memoir about what it feels like to be a chef. It's simply a collection of lessons and recipes designed to work properly, taste delicious, and help you get a good meal in front of your family.

I'm sharing what I've learned in twenty-three years at the stove about feeding people well and enjoying yourself in the process. The recipes run the gamut from simple snacks to holiday feasts; from my formula for making a proper vinaigrette to a foolproof technique for braising meat. My aim throughout is to impart a set of broader kitchen skills that will turn you, little by little, into the kind of confident, intuitive cook who can cruise a grocery aisle with purpose, and knows what to do with a fridge full of food just by rummaging through it.

This is the cookbook that I'd hand to any of my mates looking for tasty, no bullshit food that's going to be better than whatever he can warm up out of the freezer or order for takeout. Sometimes it's about a quick meal, thrown together on the fly—mushrooms on toast or a lamb burger charred up nicely on the grill. But when you have some time to tinker, I'll show you how to roast a pig's head to glistening, golden perfection, cure your own duck prosciutto, and put up jars of a silky, savory caramelized onion compote that you can slather on pretty much anything for a crazy flavor boost. Over time, you'll grow into a solid, intuitive cook—just wait and see. So go ahead; roll up your sleeves and let's get cooking.

A SHANDY WHILE YOU COOK

Most people who meet my missus are quite jealous when they hear that her husband is a chef. They must think that I come home from a seventy-hour workweek, pull on the old apron, and start boiling stocks, cracking lobsters, harvesting the home garden, and milking the dairy cow that we keep tied up out back.

The truth is that by the time my day off rolls around, I'm usually knackered and want nothing more than to enjoy my limited time with my family, eating good but simple food and having a laugh together. Whether or not you cook for a living, I can imagine that the feeling is the same. Work is hard. Feeding your family ought to be easy.

Home cooking and restaurant cooking couldn't be more different. At the restaurant we're under tremendous pressure, with ten to fifteen cooks working flat-out to produce dishes that will be memorable and worthy of the considerable investment it takes these days to dine out. Needless to say, sipping on a cocktail while you work is out of the question.

At home, it's a different story. My only goal is to make something fresh and wholesome for the people I love, without taking myself too seriously in the process. On these occasions, there is no better beverage than the shandy. Half lager, half lemon soda, the shandy is a family drink: mellow, refreshing, and light enough on the alcohol that it won't put this tired chef immediately to sleep.

SERVES 1

Half-pint Sprite or 7-Up (in England we call these lemonades, and my favorite is R. White's)

Half-pint of your favorite beer (pilsners work best)

1. Pour the lemonade into a pint glass and stir with a spoon to release some of the carbonation.

2. Pour the beer on top.

3. Drink quickly, then repeat steps 1 and 2.

1

THE KITCHEN TOOLKIT

THE RECIPES IN THIS BOOK USE VERY LITTLE IN THE WAY OF SPECIALTY EQUIPMENT, and that's intentional: I'd rather you invest in good-quality basics than stuff your kitchen full of every last strawberry huller, fondue kit, bread machine, panini press, and electric peppermill.

Below is an accounting of everything you need to make all the recipes in this book, listed roughly in order of importance. For the pricier items, like stainless steel or copper cookware, I highly recommend having a look through discount stores like T.J. Maxx and Marshalls. You can often find products from reputable brands like Cuisinart, All-Clad, and Calphalon there at incredible prices.

KNIVES: You're not going to get very far in the kitchen without a knife. Chefs tend to keep very expensive Japanese or German numbers, but those require frequent skilled sharpening, which is a lot for a home cook to take on. Your essential blade will be an 8- to 10-inch chef's knife, and for that I recommend one of the inexpensive ones made by Victorinox. Get a little hand sharpener and use it frequently to keep the blade in good working order, and simply replace it for around $40 if it becomes too dull to work with. The same goes for your paring knife, a 3- to 4-inch blade for small cutting and peeling jobs. You should also have a serrated knife about 8 inches in length, good for breads and any task where you'll be sawing through a tough exterior. Those don't require sharpening, so feel free to spend a bit more. A serrated paring knife comes in handy too. That covers the essentials, but there are lots of specialty knives you can buy if interested, such as a boning knife, filleting knife, petty knife, cleaver, and slicer.

CUTTING BOARDS: These should always be wooden, large enough so that bits of things aren't constantly falling off the sides, but not too large to easily position on your counter. Sharp knives get stuck in plastic boards and form grooves where bacteria settles. Glass cutting boards are the worst, dulling your knives and making a terrible sound when you work on them. Never, ever.

MIXING BOWLS: Preferably made from stainless steel, because it's light, durable, and easy to clean.

SCALE: In Europe, our recipes tend to call for ingredients by weight, so a good kitchen scale is absolutely essential. In the US, ingredients are most often listed by volume, which means you can usually get by without one. I still recommend buying one, as it does come in handy from time to time. Go with a digital scale, which will be the most accurate and easiest to use.

MEASURING CUPS AND SPOONS: One set of each. Stainless steel is ideal.

METAL SPATULA: For flipping items in a pan or on the grill.

RUBBER SPATULA: For thoroughly scraping out bowls and pans and stirring scrambled eggs in a nonstick skillet.

WOODEN SPOON: For stirring anything on the stove. Don't put these through the dishwasher, or the wood will dry and crack.

WHISK: For, well, whisking.

TONGS: The tool of choice for retrieving pasta from boiling water, turning sturdy meats and vegetables on a grill or in the pan, and several other kitchen tasks. Choose a basic stainless steel version.

KITCHEN TOWELS: Get a good stock of cotton towels and use them as you would oven mitts, as well as for cleaning surfaces, covering dough while it rises, drying salad greens, and the like. Put them through the laundry frequently.

BAKING SHEETS: It's a good idea to have a couple with rimmed edges and a couple without. Aluminum ones are fine.

PARCHMENT PAPER, PLASTIC WRAP, ALUMINUM FOIL: Always have a roll of each on hand, and don't buy the cheap stuff.

FINE-MESH SIEVE: For straining liquids. One that's 7 to 8 inches in diameter is ideal. If possible, get one with a double layer of mesh for finer straining.

COLANDER: For draining pasta and washing vegetables, including lettuce for salad. Don't buy a salad spinner! What a waste of space.

MICROPLANE GRATER: For zesting citrus and grating cheese, garlic, chocolate, ginger, and so on.

DUTCH OVEN: A heavy, enameled cast-iron pot will probably get more use than any other piece of cookware. Get one of 5- or 6-quart capacity. I like Lodge, which is half the price of the Le Creuset brand and just as good.

CAST-IRON PAN: These are naturally nonstick and hang on to heat well for powerful searing. A good diameter is 12 inches, and Lodge is the brand of choice.

SAUCEPANS: Get a small, medium, and large saucepan, plus a big stockpot. Ideally they should be made from triple-ply stainless steel. All-Clad is what we use.

ROASTING PAN: Invest in a large one, because it's always better to have slightly too much room in the pan than not enough. Splurge on a stainless steel one, or even copper, for food to cook most evenly.

BLACK STEEL FRY PAN: This is the tool of choice for pan-roasting fish. A good diameter is 9 inches.

NONSTICK SKILLET: I know that Teflon is out of vogue because of toxicity issues, but a nonstick pan of some sort is really ideal for omelets, crepes, pancakes, and even fish. Calphalon makes good ones. Wipe them out with a paper towel after use and don't scrub or scrape them, which damages the surface.

COPPER SAUTÉ PAN: Copper is expensive, but it distributes heat very evenly and heats quickly. If you buy just one copper pan, make it a 4- to 5-quart high-sided sauté pan. It can be used for practically any stovetop job, from sautéing vegetables to searing meat to making sauces.

GRILL PAN: Similar to the cast-iron pan except with ridges, if you want to achieve grill marks indoors.

FOOD PROCESSOR: This machine makes quick work of chopping and dough making; in a pinch it can be used for pureeing too, although it doesn't typically achieve results that are as smooth a job as what a good blender can do. Choose one with at least an 8-cup capacity. Cuisinart and Waring are good brands.

BLENDER: For making ultra-smooth sauces and soups (plus smoothies and margaritas). Vitamix is the brand of choice in professional kitchens; they are expensive but can blend virtually anything as smooth as a baby's bottom.

STAND MIXER: Not only very useful in mixing doughs, but can be used with various attachments for making pasta, grinding meat, and more. KitchenAid and Breville are my favorite brands.

PRESSURE COOKER: Today's digital countertop models are worlds better than the old stovetop battleaxes I'm used to. There are many good brands with all sorts of bells and whistles, so buy according to your budget.

MEAT THERMOMETER: I prefer digital versions, because analog ones need to be calibrated before each use, which can be a huge pain. We use a brand called Taylor.

CANDY THERMOMETER: Whereas a meat thermometer gives an instant temperature read, candy thermometers read temperature continuously. They are necessary for gauging oil temperature whenever you're deep-frying.

GRILL: Gas and charcoal are both fine; get whatever your taste and budget allows for.

MORTAR AND PESTLE: For grinding spices. These are typically made of granite or marble and the heavier, the better. Keep in mind that they're meant to be used in a smooth grinding motion; if you bang them together, and they will break or chip (if you drop them on your toe, God help you!).

LOAF PANS MEASURING 8½ × 4½ INCHES: Also known as 1-pound loaf pans. These are used for making breads or smaller terrines. There are very good nonstick versions now that don't require you to grease the pan before use, and those are the ones to buy.

PIE PAN: Buy one that's extra deep, 9 inches in diameter, and made of nonstick pan rather than glass or earthenware.

PEPPER GRINDER: Peppercorns should always be ground fresh, never bought preground, because their flavor dulls quickly. Buy a grinder that allows you to adjust the size of the grind.

FISH SPATULA: This specialty spatula has a razor-thin leading edge designed for getting underneath fish skin in a pan and keeping the whole fillet in one piece as you turn it. It's very helpful when pan-roasting a skin-on piece of fish.

SPIDER: This is a skimming tool made from mesh, and it's is the best choice for removing items from the fryer. Oil clings too heavily to a slotted spoon and will drip everywhere. Spiders can also be used to fish objects out of boiling water.

ROLLING PIN: Always wooden. I've used an empty wine bottle in a pinch, but a rolling pin is better.

PASTA MACHINE: The best choice is a pasta attachment for your stand mixer, which extrudes the dough and sheets and cuts it into the desired shapes. You can also get a hand-crank model made by Imperia. Those are cool and old school but take forever.

TERRINE DISH: These heavy earthenware or metal containers are good exclusively for making terrines such as the Smoked Salmon and Potato Terrine (page 84) and Duck and Walnut Terrine (page 97). A loaf pan works if you don't want to invest in one.

PASTRY BAGS AND METAL TIPS: A pack of large disposable bags and a few plain round tips, for piping fillings into things like Fried Squash Blossoms (page 68) and Sriracha Deviled Eggs (page 61).

MEAT GRINDER ATTACHMENT: This connects to your stand mixer and is necessary for the Duck and Walnut Terrine (page 97).

ICE CREAM MACHINE: Some sort of ice cream apparatus is essential if you want to make Eggnog Ice Cream (page 169). Options range from basic manual devices that you stir by hand to fully automatic ones with their own condensers, so that no pre-chilling of the bowl is necessary. Choose whatever's right for your level of ice cream enthusiasm. Don't spent hundreds of dollars on a machine you're going to use twice.

FRYER: A countertop fryer isn't a necessity, but it takes the guesswork (and much of the risk and mess) out of deep-frying. Breville makes a nice model.

THE OTHER TOOLKIT

LIFESAVER FLAVORS

MOST COOKBOOKS HIDE THE CONDIMENT RECIPES IN THE BACK, LUMPED IN with all the sauces and stocks that you can pretty much guarantee nobody will ever use. That's a bloody shame, because it's my opinion that great condiments—pickles, preserves, vinegars, oils, and the like—are the flavor boosters that mean the difference between a mediocre plate and a spectacular one. Experienced cooks know that a fillet of fresh striped bass with a lovely knob of homemade lemon butter can knock your socks off harder than a meal that takes hours to make, filled with all kinds of fancy footwork. Stock your fridge with a few killer homemade condiments, which can be made in batches and kept for weeks or even months, and the cooking is already halfway done.

Before you get all pumped up with DIY spirit, keep in mind that not everything is worth the effort to make from scratch. The recipes in this chapter focus your effort only where it's going to pay off big-style. For instance, mayonnaise is best left to the good people at Hellmann's/Best Foods, who make a product that's probably better than anything you're going to whip up from eggs and oil in your own kitchen. Same goes for Dijon-style mustard. Let Grey Poupon or Maille do the work for you.

PICKLED MUSTARD SEEDS

These are a nice alternative to spreadable mustard. You get that spicy, tart mustard flavor plus a little crunchy texture as the seeds pop in your mouth. Use them on sandwiches or add a big spoonful to a charcuterie board or cheese plate. They'll keep in the fridge for six months at minimum, so don't worry about whether you'll make it through the whole batch. By the way: the term *pickle* simply means to preserve something in vinegar or brine, the latter of which is a solution made from salt and water.

MAKES 3 CUPS

1 cup yellow mustard seeds

1 cup white wine vinegar, preferably Chardonnay

¾ cup water

¾ cup mirin

½ cup sugar

1 tablespoon kosher salt

1. Take a small saucepan and add the mustard seeds plus enough cold water to cover them, then place it over high heat. Once the water has reached a boil, remove the pan from the heat and strain the mustard seeds through a fine sieve. Repeat this process, known as *blanching*, twice more, using fresh cold water each time.

2. Place the blanched mustard seeds, vinegar, water, mirin, sugar, and salt in a small saucepan and bring the mixture to a simmer over low heat. Cook uncovered until the seeds are plump and tender, about 1 hour. If too much liquid evaporates, add just enough water to cover the seeds.

3. Remove the seeds from the heat, cool them to room temperature, and store them in a clean jar in the refrigerator.

CARAMELIZED ONION COMPOTE

Onion compote is one of the most perfect things there is in life. This is no exaggeration. It's got salt, sweetness from the onions and brown sugar, sourness from the vinegar, *umami* that develops during the long, slow cooking process, and bitterness from that little bit of charring that's inevitable whenever you're cooking onions in a pan. It can be used both hot and cold. It can be made with little effort and keeps for two weeks. And it works on practically anything: on sandwiches, with steak, in salads, on a charcuterie board, inside an omelet, on top of a hot dog. It's perfect alongside a piece of grilled swordfish. You can chop it up and add it to tuna tartar. I've even pureed it and added it to sauces.

Below is my basic onion compote recipe; you can customize it depending on the use. If you're going to do it with roast beef, add a little horseradish. Spoon in some Dijon mustard if you plan to serve it with pork, or add a little wasabi to customize it for salmon. If you want a little more texture, add mustard seeds. You can always add soy sauce along with the vinegar to make it really savory. With the addition of beef stock, you've got a base for French onion soup. See what I'm talking about? It's the world's best condiment.

MAKES 1 CUP

½ cup extra-virgin olive oil

2 pounds white onions, thinly sliced

1 tablespoon brown sugar

½ bottle stout or porter beer

2 tablespoons beef stock

1 tablespoon balsamic vinegar

Kosher salt and freshly cracked pepper

1. Heat the oil in a large, heavy-bottomed saucepan set over medium-high heat until it shimmers. Add in the onions and brown sugar, stir to coat them with oil, and spread them evenly in the pan. Reduce the heat to medium-low and cook, stirring occasionally, until you smell the sugars release and they become soft and translucent, 30 to 45 minutes.

2. Chuck in all the liquids and cook until they're three quarters reduced, continuing to stir the onions regularly—or else they'll burn and taste like shit. Season the mixture with a good grind of pepper and a teaspoon or two of salt, to taste. Remove the onions from the heat and set aside to let cool completely.

3. Load the onions into jars and close them tightly. The compote will keep in the fridge for around to 2 weeks . . . if it lasts that long.

PRESERVED LEMONS

The hardest thing about this recipe is the patience it takes to wait thirty days for the incredible cured lemon skins that turn up at the end. Since I'm not known for my patience, I make a big batch once a month so that I never run out.

What's so great about preserved lemons? The salt-sugar rub really mellows them, pulling out all the bitterness and leaving just bright, sunny lemon flavor. If you're wondering how to use them, the better question is how can't you use them. Chop up the skin and toss it into stews or grain salads, blend it into salad dressings, and sprinkle it on fish or chicken for starters.

MAKES 6 PRESERVED LEMONS

6 Meyer lemons

½ cup kosher salt

½ cup sugar

4 bay leaves

1 cup fresh lemon juice

1. Gently scrub the lemons under cold water. Using a sharp paring knife, score each lemon 6 times down the length of the fruit, cutting deep into the flesh but keeping the lemons intact.

2. Mix together the salt and sugar. Snip the bay leaves with a pair of scissors and add to the salt and sugar mixture. Squeeze each lemon gently to open up your incisions, then rub the salt-sugar mixture into the fruit liberally.

3. Press the lemons into two sterilized 8-ounce mason jars, cover with lemon juice, and close them up tight.

4. Refrigerate for at least 30 days (and up to 6 months). To use, slip the skin off the lemon flesh and slice it as needed. You can give the skin a quick rinse if you want, but I like to use them with a bit of the nice salt rub on them. Don't try to use the lemon flesh, though, as that is really punishingly salty.

SPICY PICKLES

Most store-bought pickles are loaded with artificial colors, industrial-grade salts, and surfactants. (What's a surfactant? Yeah, exactly.) So right there, the pickles you make yourself are going to be way better than something you buy at the grocery store. Don't shove them to the back of the fridge and forget about them, though: although technically pickles don't really go bad, they're at their freshest, crispest, and most delicious for only about a month (same goes for bought pickles). Aside from the traditional cuke version, you can also use this pickling liquid to preserve cauliflower, beets, carrots— any vegetable that's sturdy enough to sit in liquid for a long while.

MAKES THREE 20-OUNCE JARS

2 cups warm water

1¾ cups distilled
white vinegar

2 dried chipotle chiles

½ cup sugar

8 garlic cloves, sliced

1½ tablespoons kosher salt

1½ teaspoons celery seeds

½ teaspoon crushed
red pepper

12 Kirby cucumbers

1. Combine the water, vinegar, chiles, sugar, garlic, salt, celery seeds, and crushed red pepper in a large bowl. Stir and let stand at room temperature for 2 hours, or until the sugar and salt are dissolved.

2. Divide the cucumbers among three 20-ounce wide-mouth mason jars. Cover them with the pickling liquid.

3. Close the jars tightly and refrigerate them for at least 10 days and up to 1 month.

HERBY PICKLES

As if you need another reason to love pickles: they happen to be really good for you. Vinegar aids digestion by keeping yeast levels in check in your gut, improves blood sugar levels, and keeps your metabolism up. A pickle a day keeps the doctor away!

MAKES 4 QUARTS

4 pounds pickling cucumbers, such as Kirby

½ cup kosher salt

10 cups white wine vinegar

2 cups water

1 teaspoon allspice berries

1 teaspoon cracked white peppercorns

1 teaspoon cracked black peppercorns

4 sprigs each dill, parsley, chervil, tarragon, and basil

1 tablespoon sugar in the raw

½ cup chopped shallots

1. Split the cucumbers in half lengthwise, sprinkle the cut surfaces evenly with half of the salt, and let them sit for 30 to 45 minutes. This extracts water from the cucumbers and allows them to pickle more deeply.

2. In a large pan set over high heat, combine the rest of the salt, the vinegar, water, allspice, peppercorns, herbs, sugar, and shallots. Bring to a boil, then remove from the heat. Let the pickling liquid cool to room temperature, then refrigerate it until cold.

3. Divide the cucumbers among four 1-quart wide-mouth mason jars and cover them in pickling liquid. Seal them. Leave them in the fridge for about a week before digging in. They'll keep for up to 6 weeks.

SWEET CHILI MARMALADE

This recipe is a secret weapon of mine, frankly a lazy fix for any dish that needs a quick shot in the arm. The combination of sweet, heat, and salt is positively addictive. Use it anywhere you'd put hot sauce. So, pretty much everywhere.

MAKES 3 PINT JARS

12 red Fresno chiles, coarsely chopped

One finger-sized piece fresh ginger, peeled and coarsely chopped

8 garlic cloves, peeled

1 pound cherry tomatoes

3 cups plus 2 tablespoons light brown sugar

1 cup red wine vinegar

1. Chuck the chiles (seeds and all), ginger, and garlic into a food processor and pulse the stuff until it's very finely chopped.

2. Scrape the chile mixture into a heavy-bottomed pan with the tomatoes, brown sugar, and vinegar. Bring to a boil over medium-high heat, skimming off any scummy looking stuff that comes to the surface. Turn the heat down to a slow simmer. Cook uncovered for about 1 hour, stirring occasionally.

3. When the marmalade becomes sticky, continue cooking for 10 to 15 minutes more, stirring frequently so that it doesn't fucking burn—otherwise you've just wasted your time. It should now look like thick, bubbling lava.

4. Remove the pan from the heat and once it has cooled off slightly, pour it into sterilized mason jars. Close them up tightly and process in a water bath. (For best practices on food safety, consult the USDA guidelines at nchfp.uga.edu and note that processing time may vary depending on your altitude and the size of your jar.) Store up to 3 months in a cool, dark cupboard or in the refrigerator.

WALNUT MUSTARD

There was a period of six months when I was on a total mustard craze. I was grinding my own mustard seed, experimenting with different styles and colors, tinkering with pickling techniques, working in different flavors and textures. In the end I only got two thoroughly enjoyable recipes out of the obsession, but that's how it goes with these things. They can't all be winners.

This recipe came about as an accompaniment for duck pâté. I wanted the pâté to be somewhat sweet, so the walnuts and vinegar were there for bitterness and acidity to balance the flavors. It turns out that walnut mustard is great not only with pâté but also on cheese plates and sandwiches, and I even stir it into a butter sauce for roast halibut or chicken.

MAKES 1½ CUPS

2 tablespoons walnuts

**6 tablespoons
Dijon mustard**

**6 tablespoons
grainy mustard**

**¼ cup white wine vinegar,
preferably Chardonnay**

**Salt and freshly ground
black pepper**

4 tablespoons walnut oil

1. Preheat the oven to 325°F.

2. Spread the walnuts in a single layer on a baking sheet. Toast them until golden and fragrant, about 5 minutes.

3. Place the walnuts in a pestle bowl and break them down with a mortar until the largest pieces are about the size of a cracked peanut. Add the Dijon mustard and continue mixing. Add the grainy mustard and vinegar, mixing still. Add a small amount of salt and pepper at this point.

4. Now slowly add the walnut oil in a fine drizzle while continuing to mix; the final product should have the texture of chunky peanut butter. Taste, and add salt and pepper as desired.

ROMESCO SAUCE

This classic Spanish recipe is traditionally used as a dipping sauce for vegetables, but I think it's just too good to confine to one purpose. I sometimes smear it on top of a firm white fish like halibut or sole before baking, or serve it alongside grilled meats. Romesco keeps for about a week in the fridge if you hold back the parsley and add that right before serving. And a word about seasoning: always taste food for salt at the same temperature you'll be eating it. Everything tastes saltier when hot, so it may need a dash more salt once cooled.

MAKES 2 CUPS

4 large garlic cloves

10 tablespoons olive oil

1 (1-inch) slice baguette

3 tablespoons almonds

3 tablespoons hazelnuts

2 medium shallots, sliced

½ teaspoon smoked paprika

4 ounces piquillo peppers

6 tablespoons Tomato Confit (page 31)

1 teaspoon tomato paste

2 tablespoons red wine vinegar

2 tablespoons water

Salt and freshly ground black pepper

2 tablespoons chopped fresh parsley

Juice of ½ lemon

1. First, blanch the garlic: fill a small saucepan two thirds full with cold water and bring it to a boil. Toss in the garlic and cook for 2 minutes, then drain it in a colander or mesh sieve.

2. Add 2 tablespoons of the oil to a medium skillet set over medium heat. Fry the slice of baguette until golden brown all over, about 2 minutes on each side. Remove it from the pan.

3. Add the almonds and hazelnuts to the same pan and toast them until golden and fragrant, 2 to 3 minutes. Remove them from the pan and add another 2 tablespoons oil, followed by the shallots and garlic. Reduce the heat to medium-low and sweat the garlic and shallots, stirring them frequently; continue until they smell sweet and are completely translucent, 4 to 5 minutes. Add the paprika and cook for 1 minute more.

4. Stir in the piquillo peppers, confit tomatoes, and tomato paste and cook for another minute. Add the vinegar and scrape up any browned bits stuck to the pan (this is called *deglazing*). Add the toasted nuts and bread back to the pan and cook for 1 minute, stirring.

5. Dump the contents of the pan into a food processor and blend until smooth. With the food processor running, add the remaining 6 tablespoons oil in a steady stream, followed by the water. Taste it, and season it to your liking with salt and pepper. Transfer to a bowl and let cool.

6. Add the parsley and lemon juice and adjust the salt to taste.

TOMATO CONFIT

These roasted, oil-packed tomatoes are good for lots of uses: on sandwiches, mixed into risotto, as a condiment with steak or salmon—anywhere you want a really intense tomato flavor. The tomatoes and herbs infuse the oil too, which is delicious in its own right. Try tossing spaghetti with diced confit tomatoes and a bit of their oil in place of making a sauce.

Getting the peel off tomatoes can be a huge pain in the ass. The key here is straight-up selection. What you're looking for is bright green vines and stems, even coloring, no breaks in the skin, and a really fragrant herbal smell. The tomato should be red; not pink, not greenish, but red. It's always best to use local tomatoes when they're in season, but we're concentrating the flavor so much in this recipe that any ripe tomatoes will work.

MAKES 1 QUART

3 pounds vine-ripe tomatoes

2 garlic cloves, thinly sliced

1 sprig rosemary

4 to 5 leaves fresh basil

1 cup extra-virgin olive oil

Sea salt

1. Fill a stockpot two thirds full with water and bring it to a boil over high heat. Fill a large bowl with ice water.

2. Dig the eye out of the top of each tomato with a paring knife, then score a cross into the opposite end. Working 4 or 5 at a time, drop the tomatoes into the boiling water. Remove them after exactly 10 seconds using a slotted spoon and immediately transfer them to the ice water. Repeat until all the tomatoes are blanched. The peel should now separate easily from the tomato.

3. Remove the tomatoes from the ice water, discard the peel, and cut them in half (top to bottom, not through the middle).

4. Place the tomatoes cut-side down on a nonreactive baking sheet (aluminum, steel, copper, or iron all make tomatoes taste metallic. If you have baking sheets made of any of these metals, which almost everyone does, line them with parchment paper to avoid this effect).

5. Preheat the oven to 180°F.

6. Place a slice of garlic, a few rosemary needles, and a small piece of torn basil on top of each tomato half, then drizzle with a touch of oil and sprinkle them with salt. Transfer the sheet to the oven and roast for 90 minutes. Turn off the heat and leave them in the oven for an additional hour, then remove them and cool to room temperature.

7. Carefully place the tomatoes and their juices in a 1-quart jar and cover them with the remaining oil; make sure they are fully submerged in oil to keep them from oxidizing and going bad. Close the jar and refrigerate for 10 to 14 days.

PICKLED RED ONIONS

I've loved pickled onions ever since I was a kid. Down at the chip shop, there were jars of golf ball-sized pickling onions soaked in malt vinegar; this is a traditional pairing with fish and chips, good for cutting through all that grease. And in the gastronomically remedial Britain of the 1980s, a little piece of cheddar and a silver-skinned cocktail onion stuck through with a toothpick was a popular hors d'oeuvre. But if you weren't brought up on the flavor, English pickled onions can taste a bit harsh, as they're soaked in straight vinegar. My recipe incorporates sugar and spices to balance the flavor a bit and take the edge off. These are a great way introduce a little acid to sandwiches or salads.

MAKES 5 CUPS

**2 pounds red onions
(3 medium or 2 large),
thinly sliced**

1½ cups white wine vinegar

½ cup sugar

½ cinnamon stick

5 cloves

1 bay leaf

1 star anise

Dash of chile flakes

1. First, blanch the onions: Fill a medium saucepan two thirds full with cold water and bring it to a boil. Toss in the red onions and cook for 2 minutes, then drain them in a colander or mesh sieve.

2. Meanwhile, in a separate saucepan, combine the vinegar, sugar, cinnamon, cloves, bay leaf, star anise, and chile flakes. Bring to a boil over high heat, then reduce it to a simmer. Cover and simmer for 5 minutes. Add the blanched onions and simmer for 1 minute more.

3. Transfer the onions and liquid to a glass jar and cool to room temperature. Close them up tight and store in the refrigerator for up to several weeks.

INFUSED OILS AND VINEGARS

One thing that oils and vinegars have in common is they're both great at taking on flavor and locking it in ready-to-deploy form. Infusing them with herbs, spices, fruit zests, and so on is simple, and such a good way to add dimension to your cooking that it would be cruel not to include them in a book of this nature. Here are a few sample recipes, but I encourage you to raid the spice cabinet and produce aisle and do as your heart desires. Just remember not to heat olive oil above 120°F, because it burns easily and will develop an off flavor, and when infusing either oil or vinegar with soft ingredients like fresh fruits, vegetables, and herbs, too much heat will cause them to break apart and turn the liquid cloudy and unappealing.

CITRUS OIL
MAKES 1 PINT

1 teaspoon coriander seeds

2 cups olive oil

Peel of 1 lemon, pith removed

Peel of 1 lime, pith removed

Peel of 1 orange, pith removed

1. In a small saucepan over medium heat, toast the coriander seeds until golden, fragrant, and starting to pop. Reduce the heat to medium-low, add the oil, and gently bring the temperature to 120°F (about the temperature of bathwater).

2. Add the citrus peels and pour the mixture into a bottle or jar. Allow it to steep at room temperature for 2 hours; use immediately or keep refrigerated for up to a month.

SPICY HERB AND GARLIC OIL
MAKES 1 PINT

2 cups olive oil

4 garlic cloves, smashed and peeled

4 whole dried chiles, such as árbol or bird's eye

2 sprigs each thyme, rosemary, and tarragon

2 fresh sage leaves

1. In a small saucepan over medium-low heat, combine the oil, garlic, chiles, and herbs, and gently bring the oil temperature to 120°F (about the temperature of bathwater).

2. Pour the mixture into a bottle or jar. Allow it to steep at room temperature for 2 hours; use immediately or keep refrigerated for up to 1 month.

(continued)

CHILE VINEGAR
MAKES 1 QUART

4 cups rice wine vinegar
1 fresh habanero chile
1 fresh jalapeño chile
1 dried chipotle chile
2 shallots, thinly sliced
1 small bunch cilantro

1. Place all the ingredients in a clean 1-quart mason jar and close the lid tightly.

2. Fill a stockpot two thirds full with water and bring it to a boil. Using a pair of kitchen tongs, place the jar into the water carefully and continue to boil for 1 hour. Remove the jar and let it cool. The vinegar will stay good for months; just a heads up: it will continue to generate heat and flavor from the chiles as it ages.

BLACKBERRY-ANISE VINEGAR
MAKES 1 QUART

4 cups red wine vinegar
1 pint blackberries
3 star anise
3 sprigs tarragon

1. Place all the ingredients in a clean 1-quart mason jar and close the lid tightly.

2. Fill a stockpot two thirds full with water and bring it to a boil. Using a pair of kitchen tongs, place the jar into the water carefully and continue to boil for 1 hour. Remove the jar and allow it to infuse for 24 hours at room temperature, then remove the star anise. After about a week, this vinegar is stunning both in flavor and color. The vinegar will stay good for months; when using it, avoid the solid ingredients and use the liquid only.

HERB BUTTER

Compound butters—aka butter mixed with tasty bits—are dead easy to make, and they are a simple way to add a quick hit of flavor to meats, fish, vegetables, and so on. I've always got at least a couple of different versions knocking about in my freezer, where they keep for months. This simple herb butter is a tasty basic example, but you can flavor butter with pretty much anything you want (any sort of herb or spice, sugars, cheeses, chiles—you name it), so let your imagination run wild.

MAKES 1 POUND BUTTER

1 pound (4 sticks) unsalted butter, preferably Kerrygold or Lurpak (don't buy the cheap stuff; you get what you pay for)

3 tablespoons fresh lemon juice, from about 2 lemons

2 garlic cloves, minced to a fine paste with a Microplane

2 heaping tablespoons finely chopped fresh flat-leaf parsley

Salt and freshly ground black pepper

1. Allow the butter to soften. If you're too disorganized to take it out of the fridge an hour or so before you need it, then cut it into small chunks and chuck it in the microwave for 5 seconds at a time until soft. Be careful not to let it melt, because you can't un-melt butter.

2. In a large bowl using a plastic spatula, beat the butter vigorously for a minute or two until it reaches a creamy, cake frosting-like texture. This is pretty hard work, kind of a chef's version of going at a speed bag. It helps to think of somebody you don't like.

3. Add the lemon juice, garlic, and parsley and continue the beat the butter until the ingredients are fully mixed. Season with salt and pepper.

4. Spread out a square of plastic wrap at least 12 inches long across your work surface, then scoop the mixed butter onto the plastic. Roll the butter into a cylinder inside the plastic wrap. Tie the ends of the plastic wrap into knots so that you have an enclosed, sausage-like cylinder of butter. Chill or freeze until needed. Slice off disks of butter for use on the tabletop or in cooking, being sure to reseal the butter well before returning it to the refrigerator or freezer.

3

THINGS ON BREAD

MAN FOOD IN A PINCH

LEGEND HAS IT THAT SANDWICHES ORIGINATED IN BRITAIN IN THE EIGHTEENTH century, the brainchild of John Montagu, Earl of Sandwich. As a result, the sandwich has been called Britain's biggest contribution to gastronomy. I only wish we could rightfully claim this culinary masterwork, which I would personally rank above the steam engine, telephone, and lightbulb in the scheme of British inventions. But the reality is, the idea of putting things between bread—whether or not you call it a sandwich—is ancient and universal, from the *bánh mì* of Vietnam to France's *croquet-monsieur*, Malaysia's *roti*, and Greece's gyros.

Men have a particular affinity for sandwiches, and I think that's because we're not shy about eating with our hands and letting things dribble down our chins. The almighty sandwich is one of the first foods I learned to love. After twenty-five years of working my arse off in kitchens, I can now cook myself virtually anything, but sandwiches remain a tent-pole of my home cooking repertoire. I love them for their utter simplicity and range: a sandwich makes sense at any time of day, from a bacon and egg number at breakfast to the grilled cheese you fire up as a late-night snack. Once you understand the basics of putting flavors and textures together, you can feed yourself well in almost any situation. This chapter will teach you how.

MUSHROOMS ON TOAST

Whether for breakfast, lunch, or a late-night snack, this open-faced sandwich is a real melting pot of flavors, one of those dishes with a good meaty feeling to it but little actual meat. All kinds of mushrooms work; if it's springtime and you can get your hands on porcinis or chanterelles, they're really the cream of the crop. But readily available options like oysters, shiitakes, portobellos, and creminis will do just fine.

When you get mushrooms home from the store, keep them in the refrigerator between paper towels or in a brown paper bag. Most mushrooms that you buy are cultivated, not picked wild, so you don't even need to wash them before use. If there's any visible dirt, wipe it off with a damp towel. You really want to avoid submerging them in water, as mushrooms are like sponges and will soak up any liquid you put them in.

SERVES 2 (IF YOU'RE HUNGRY) OR 4 (FOR A SNACK)

4 slices sourdough bread, just shy of 1-inch thick

1 tablespoon olive oil

4 slices prosciutto

2 tablespoons soy sauce

2 tablespoons yuzu juice or lemon juice

¼ teaspoon wasabi paste

1½ teaspoons toasted sesame oil

4 tablespoons (½ stick) unsalted butter plus a knob for frying the eggs

4 large organic eggs

12 ounces mixed wild mushrooms

1 garlic clove, crushed

2 tablespoon sliced scallions, white and pale green parts only

Handful of fresh parsley leaves, finely chopped

Salt and freshly ground black pepper

1. Toast the bread, cut each slice in half, and set them aside. Heat a large skillet over medium-high heat and add the oil. Once the oil is hot, add the prosciutto and fry until golden and crisp, about 2 minutes per side. Break the crispy ham into large pieces and set it aside on paper towels.

2. In a small bowl, whisk together the soy sauce, yuzu, wasabi, and sesame oil.

3. In a separate skillet, melt the knob of butter over medium heat. Add the eggs and fry until they're as well-cooked as you like them (I like the whites just opaque and the yolks super runny). Transfer them from the pan to a plate and set aside.

4. Turn the heat up to medium-high and add the remaining 4 tablespoons butter. Let the butter cook until nut brown and beginning to smoke, then add the mushrooms. Leave them alone for at least a minute—that's how they'll get a nice deep, meaty sear—then give them a stir and cook them a minute more. Add the garlic and scallions and continue to cook for 3 to 5 minutes.

5. Add the soy-yuzu dressing and cook until the liquid is reduced to a glossy, viscous sauce. Stir in half of the parsley, taste the mixture, and add more salt if necessary and some pepper. Pile the mushrooms high on the toasts and top them with the prosciutto, fried eggs, and more fresh parsley.

THE PERFECT SANDWICH, EVERY TIME

I've included a few sandwich recipes in this chapter to give you the blueprints for some of my favorite combinations. To tell you the truth, though, relying on recipes for sandwiches is kind of like reading your half of a conversation from a script. Sandwiches are almost always best when you make them up on the fly, adapting to whatever ingredients you find yourself faced with.

First of all, you can't make a great sandwich out of shitty ingredients. It's just not possible. You can't build a Porsche out of old Pontiac parts. So—not to sound like a complete prat—but let the ingredients speak to you. What looks the best in the supermarket, farmers' market, bodega, convenience store, or wherever else you're shopping? Really fresh cucumbers, salt, and mayonnaise on toast is going to make for a better lunch than a ham and cheese sandwich if all you can find is slimy, pre-packaged cold cuts and Kraft singles.

Resist the urge to overdo it. You want to be able to taste each ingredient on the sandwich, rather than slathering on a bunch of random relishes and spreads and setting up a flavor death match. Less is more. To me the perfect sandwich is a *jambon beurre*, the French classic made from really good crusty baguette, a thin layer of ham, and high-quality butter. It's just three ingredients, and it couldn't be better.

Balancing textures is also important. If you're using a hard rustic bread, for instance, you've got to make sure that everything inside is easy to chew. Add something really sturdy like roast beef and you'll burn out your jaw. On the flipside, a combination like egg salad on white bread is going to make you feel like you're eating lunch in an old folks' home. You've also got to think about the way the whole thing swallows. If you've got a lot of dry textures together—crusty bread, chicken breast, cheddar, for example—you'll end up drinking water to get a bite down, which really kills the flavor.

Remember practicalities too. You want to be able to eat the thing without detaching your jaw, so don't make it four inches thick. And there is nothing worse than biting into a sandwich and having it fall apart in your hands. Make sure the bread can stand up to your fillings.

Last, if you make a sandwich in advance, the best thing to wrap it in is waxed paper. Avoid aluminum foil and plastic wrap, because the sandwich will get nasty and soggy if it can't breathe. Don't put any wet ingredients—washed lettuce, condiments, tomatoes—directly against the bread, or in a matter of an hour or two the bread will go to shit.

GRILLED SKIRT STEAK AND HORSERADISH SANDWICH

Skirt steak is the ideal sandwich cut. It's cheap, fast, and easy to cook, tender enough that you won't put your jaw out trying to bite through it, and it has a rich, intense flavor of beef to it. It's also a naturally slim piece of meat, no more than ½ inch thick and about 4 inches wide, which makes it the perfect dimensions for laying a slab between two slices of bread. Adding the heat of horseradish, creamy mayo, and peppery arugula rounds out the flavors perfectly. If you think you like roast beef sandwiches made with gray deli roast beef, just wait. You'll go nuts for this.

SERVES 2

12 ounces skirt steak

½ cup Skirt Steak Marinade (recipe follows)

Kosher salt

2 slices ciabatta bread, about 6 × 4 inches, sliced down the middle

2 tablespoons unsalted butter, softened

⅓ cup mayonnaise

1½ tablespoons prepared horseradish (or more, to suit your taste)

2 handfuls of arugula

Freshly ground black pepper

1. Trim any excess fat off the steak, rub it with the marinade, and place it in a zip-top bag or covered container in the refrigerator for at least 2 but no more than 8 hours; more than that and the meat will turn mushy when it cooks.

2. Fire up the grill and let it get hot, or place a grill pan or cast-iron pan or over high heat for 5 minutes. Remove the steak from the marinade, scrape off any excess herbs and garlic, season it liberally with salt, then grill the meat to your liking. Medium-rare will take about 1 minute per side.

3. Toast the bread if you want, or simply butter the bloody stuff. In a small bowl, mix together the mayonnaise and horseradish to your desired spiciness.

4. Build up your sandwich by slathering the horseradish mayo on the bottom slice of bread, then put down a bed of arugula, followed by your meat, freshly ground pepper, and the top slice of bread.

SKIRT STEAK MARINADE
MAKES ABOUT ½ CUP

½ cup olive oil

1 tablespoon chopped garlic

1 tablespoon chopped fresh thyme

1 tablespoon chopped fresh parsley

1 tablespoon chopped fresh rosemary

2 tablespoons Sprite or 7-Up (the phosphoric acid will tenderize the meat to melt in the mouth)

Zest of ½ lemon

Dump all the ingredients in a blender and blend until combined.

STILTON AND ONION MARMALADE GRILLED CHEESE

Stilton is not exactly your classic grilling cheese, but it's one of our proudest British exports and it's funky and terrific paired with rich, buttery brioche. Give it a chance!

Let's talk grilled cheese basics, because no matter what kind of cheese or bread you use, the procedure is going to be the same. The biggest mistake people make with grilled cheese is getting the pan too hot, which means the bread burns before everything inside turns warm and gooey. Keep the heat low and slow. Along the same lines, if you get greedy and pile the cheese on too heavily, it won't melt through; ⅛ to ¼ inch in thickness is ideal. When it comes to bread, the softer the better, and don't use anything with bits of whole grain, nuts, or fruits, all of which will burn. Always spread the outside of the bread with soft butter, which is key to achieving that crisp, golden exterior.

SERVES 1

2 tablespoons unsalted butter, softened

2 (¾-inch thick) slices of brioche

2½ ounces sliced Stilton or other creamy, not crumbly, blue cheese

⅓ cup Caramelized Onion Compote (page 21)

1. Lightly butter both sides of both slices of bread; the bread and cheese both have a lot of fat in them already, so don't go too crazy.

2. Spread the inside of both slices of bread with the onion compote and place the cheese evenly in the middle.

3. Heat a black steel, Teflon, or cast-iron pan—something the bread won't stick to—over medium-low heat. Cook the sandwich until the bread is golden brown and the cheese begins to turn soft and warm, 3 to 4 minutes, then flip it and repeat on the other side. Slice in half and eat immediately.

OPEN-FACED PORK LOIN SANDWICH WITH BUTTER LETTUCE

I know there's something a bit dainty and foofoo about the idea of an open-faced sandwich, but even though I really enjoy bread—everything about it, from weighing the ingredients to kneading it, shaping it, baking it, smelling it, and most of all eating the stuff—it does have a nasty tendency to fill you up. Removing one slice from the sandwich equation can improve your bread-to-meat ratio, bringing all the ingredients back into balance. Try this one on for size and see what you think. It's a great recipe to scale up and make for a whole army of people: buy a 2- to 3-pound pork loin and roast it, get a couple loaves of great bread, and lay all the ingredients out in serve-yourself fashion.

SERVES 2

6 ounces center-cut pork loin

Pork Brine (recipe follows)

2 big slices of hearty bread, such as baguette or sourdough

2 tablespoons unsalted butter, softened

½ recipe Butter Lettuce Salad (page 121)

2 Herby Pickles (page 25)

1. In a zip-top bag or covered container, combine the pork and brine and let it sit in the refrigerator for at least 2 but ideally 4 hours. Give the pork a quick wash and dry it with paper towels.

2. Preheat the oven to 375°F.

3. Place the pork in a small metal or glass pan and roast it until the internal temperature of the meat reaches 135°F, around 10 minutes (20 minutes per pound is a good guideline for pork, in case you're cooking a bigger piece of meat). Remove the meat from the oven and let it rest for 10 minutes.

4. Toast the bread if you like, then butter it generously. Slice the pork as thinly as possible. Top the bread with a thick layer of pork, top that with the butter lettuce salad, and serve with a pickle on the side.

PORK BRINE
MAKES 2 CUPS

2 cups water

1 tablespoon salt

1½ teaspoons sugar

1 sprig cilantro

1 clove

1 star anise

Combine all the ingredients in a small saucepan and bring to a boil over high heat. Remove the pan from the heat and cool to room temperature.

CIABATTA

No matter what the artisan bread-baking books have told you, a lot of breads just aren't that easy to make well at home. Take baguettes, for instance, or those big, round, crusty French pains de campagne: you really need a special steam-injection oven for those to turn out right. Ciabatta is a different story. It does just fine in any oven. It's supposed to look rustic, so you can do an ugly job of shaping the loaves without feeling like you've screwed it up. Plus it's a top-notch sandwich bread, soft enough to chew easily but sturdy enough to stand up to fillings. Like any bread, it's best eaten the same day—remember, we're not adding any preservatives here—but wrapped tightly in foil, it'll be OK the day after you bake it, too. Especially toasted.

MAKES 2 LOAVES

FOR THE MOTHER

⅛ teaspoon active dry yeast

2 tablespoons warm (105 to 115°F) water

⅓ cup room-temperature water

1 cup bread flour, preferably organic

FOR THE BREAD

½ teaspoon active dry yeast

2 tablespoons warm (105 to 115°F) whole milk

⅔ cup room-temperature water

1 tablespoon olive oil, plus more for greasing

2 cups bread flour, preferably organic

1½ teaspoons salt

1. First, make the mother: In a small bowl, stir together the yeast and warm water and let sit for 5 minutes, or until it's milky and frothy. Dump this yeast slurry into a larger bowl with the room-temperature water and flour and stir the mixture until it forms a smooth paste (no flour lumps!), maybe 4 minutes. Cover the bowl with plastic wrap and leave it in a cool room for at least 12 hours. It should triple in size at least. You can keep a mother for years and she'll continue to generate flavor—you just have to keep feeding her (sparked your curiosity, have I? Check out page 50 for more information).

2. Now, make the bread: In a small bowl, stir together the yeast and warm milk and let it sit for 5 minutes, or until it's slightly frothy. In a stand mixer fitted with the dough hook, combine this yeast slurry, a fistful of the mother (that'll be a cup or so), the water, oil, and flour and mix it at low speed until the flour is just moistened. Beat the dough at medium speed for 3 minutes. Add the salt and beat the dough for 4 minutes more. Scrape the dough into a large oiled bowl and cover it tightly with plastic wrap. Let the dough rise at room temperature until it doubles in bulk, about 1½ hours. At this point, God willing, the dough will be sticky and full of air bubbles.

3. Ready 2 rimless baking sheets by covering them with well-floured sheets of parchment paper. Turn the dough out onto a floured work surface and cut it in half. Transfer each half to its own baking sheet. Working gently, lads, and trying not to knock too much air out of the dough, form the dough into rectangles about 9 × 4 inches; handle the dough as little as possible, and don't worry if the loaf shapes are uneven. Just call them "rustic." Dimple the loaves with floured fingers and dust the tops with flour. Cover the loaves with dampened kitchen towels and let them rise at room temperature until almost doubled in bulk, 1½ to 2 hours.

4. Meanwhile, preheat the oven to 425°F.

5. Bake the ciabatta loaves for 20 minutes, or until pale golden. Using a large spatula, transfer them to a rack to cool. Eat them the same day, or freeze them wrapped in foil inside a zip-top bag.

A WORD TO YOUR MOTHER

Call it a mother, a sponge, pâte fermentée, pre-ferment, or fermentation starter: if you want to make bread with seriously good flavor, the best way to do it is to add some dough that's been sitting around your kitchen for a while. And I mean a long while.

When you combine water, flour, and yeast, the yeast feeds on the flour, converting the carbs to acids and alcohols with a whole range of lovely flavors. That's fermentation. Keep giving the yeast flour and water and the fermentation will continue indefinitely, layering flavor on top of flavor. Now you have your "mother." There are people who literally pass these things down across generations.

You've got to feed the mother every couple of days to keep it alive, so it's not unlike having a pet—that means if you go away on vacation for the week, you're either going to have to give it to a friend to look after or pop it in the fridge and take your chances. Every 2 to 3 days, remove a quarter of the dough (either use it to bake bread, or just throw it away if you must) and add fresh flour and water. So, if the dough is stored in a quart-sized container, you'll remove 1 cup of dough, mix together ½ cup flour and ½ cup water, and add that in. If you want to make a sourdough, leave some pineapple juice or grapefruit juice out until it goes sour and add that instead of water.

Store the mother in a warm, dark place in a jar or plastic container large enough for it to triple in size and wrap it in plastic wrap poked through with holes so that it can breathe. Think of it as your own personal flavor factory, churning away in your pantry.

BRIOCHE

Brioche is kind of like a bread that wants to be a pastry. The dough is rich, soft, and buttery, and caramelizes really nicely when baked. As a sandwich bread, it's amazing with smoked fish and meat. I also love it in a grilled cheese with sharp, cheddary cheeses that balance out its richness.

Brioche is traditionally baked in special round tins, but those are really expensive, so back when I was working in London we came up with a cheapskate workaround: we baked the loaves in the big 2½-quart cans that restaurants get things like tomato juice and canned fruit delivered in. It's pretty hard for a home cook to get his hands on cans that large, but if you can find them, I highly recommend giving the method a try.

MAKES 2 LOAVES

4 cups unbleached all-purpose flour

⅓ cup granulated sugar

4½ teaspoons active dry yeast

2 teaspoons salt

6 large eggs, at room temperature

½ cup whole milk, at room temperature

16 tablespoons (1 cup) unsalted butter, cut into 16 pieces, softened, plus more for buttering the pans

1 large egg yolk

1. Dust off your stand mixer and fit it with the paddle attachment. Mix the flour, sugar, yeast, and salt on low speed to combine them. Add 4 of the eggs and the milk and continue mixing on low speed. Once the dough shows signs of coming together, swap out the paddle for a dough hook.

2. Mix the dough on medium speed for a couple of minutes, then scrape down the bowl and the dough hook. Mix for a couple of minutes more, or until the dough starts to look elastic, then scrape down the bowl and hook again.

3. With the mixer on medium-low speed, start adding the butter a few pieces at a time. Once all of the butter has been added, increase the speed to medium and mix for 3 to 4 minutes. Then—you guessed it!—scrape down the dough hook and bowl one more time. We're trying to make sure this dough is as evenly combined as possible. Now mix the dough again until it's smooth and shiny, 4 to 5 minutes. The dough will slap against the sides of the bowl to announce that it's ready.

4. Place the dough on a baking sheet, cover it with plastic wrap, and refrigerate for at least 2 hours and up to 24 hours. If the dough had a lengthy refrigeration time, you'll want to let it warm to room temperature before proceeding, about 2 hours. Meanwhile, butter two 8½ × 4½-inch loaf pans (these are also knows as 1-pound loaf pans).

5. Turn the dough out, top down, onto a clean, lightly floured work surface. Form the dough into a neat ball by folding the sides toward the middle. Divide it into 2 equal pieces; they should be 1 pound 3 ounces each, if you're keeping score. Drop them into the loaf pans and cover them with plastic wrap (at this stage, the brioches can be wrapped well and frozen for up to a month). Let the dough rise at room temperature until almost doubled in size, about 1½ hours. It should spring back when gently poked with a finger.

(continued)

6. Meanwhile, position an oven rack in the center of the oven and preheat it to 375°F.

7. In a small bowl, make an egg wash by beating the remaining 2 eggs and 1 egg yolk. Lightly brush the tops of the brioches without letting the egg wash drip down into the pans, which can make the loaves stick to their pans. Bake until dark golden brown on top and golden on the sides (you can lift the brioche slightly to peek in at the edge of the mold), about 18 minutes. For those who like thermometers, the internal temperature should be 190°F. Let the brioches cool on a wire rack for 10 minutes before unmolding. Eat immediately, or cool, wrap airtight, and freeze for up to a month.

HOW TO BUY BREAD

I've given you recipes for ciabatta and brioche, and I do hope you'll make them at least once if only to see what it's like. But I'm a realist. I know that week in, week out, most blokes will be buying their sandwich bread, not making it. That's perfectly fine, as long as you're smart about it.

First of all, the supermarket is usually not the best place to go buy your bread. Do not visit the aisle with those pre-sliced, plastic-wrapped, undead zombie loaves. They're full of preservatives and added gluten and God knows what that doesn't belong in bread. Bread isn't meant to stay soft for days or even weeks on end. It's unnatural. Always go the freshly baked route if you can. Some of the better grocery stores get loaves in from a good local baker, like La Brea in California or Bread Alone in New York. Those are great options.

How can you tell if you're dealing with good bread? The crust is the most important thing—it should be firm and springy. Good bread has some heft to it. If it feels hollow, then it's full of air and cheap fillers. Smell it; bread should always have a good strong whiff of yeast, which is how you know it's made with real yeast and not artificial, industrial "super proofers."

Recently here's been a big resurgence in small bakeries where you can get truly excellent loaves at a good price, while supporting a small business at the same time. Best case scenario is a local bakery that's using organic or imported flour. Not to get too political, but I really believe that all the weed killers and pesticides being sprayed on the wheat grown in the United States may well be what's making it hard for many of us to stomach bread (so then, not the gluten after all). In my house, we've gone fully organic with our bread and we're all feeling a lot healthier for it.

The reality is that fresh bread—real bread, made from flour, yeast, water, salt, and nothing else—has a very short shelf life. It just does. Don't expect it to last more than 24 to 48 hours from the time it leaves the oven. The good news is that it freezes very well, which allows you to buy 3 or 4 loaves at a time without sacrificing quality or throwing a bunch away. As soon as you get home, immediately slice what you won't eat the same day and freeze it in a zip-top bag. Now you can take slices out of the freezer on demand. And bread straight from the freezer makes the absolute best toast: crispy on the outside, tender on the inside.

THE CHIPS ARE DOWN

THERE'S NOTHING GLOOMIER THAN SITTING DOWN AT THE END OF A LONG DAY TO A tatty bag of pretzels or crisps. That's why I've put together this selection of tasty, easy-to-execute snacks that will come in handy whether it's just you and the missus, a few mates over for beers, or you're hosting a full-on dinner party. Time to toss out your old faithful Cheetos, Slim Jims, and energy bars, roll up your sleeves, and make something worth eating.

I hear it said all the time that snacking is bad for you. Snacking isn't bad for you; it's what we choose to snack on most of the time that turns us soft around the middle: the cheap shit that's full of preservatives, artificial additives, and loads of sugar. You'll notice the recipes in this chapter ain't exactly rabbit food—we're talking deviled eggs, chicharrónes, whipped lardo—but when you've made something with your own two hands, you know exactly what's in it. That's the absolute best way to look after your health. Everything doesn't always need to be mega-organic either, just as long as you use good, fresh, minimally processed ingredients. That's what this chapter is all about.

WARM MARINATED OLIVES

Great olives, ripened to perfection, cleaned of all their bitterness, and lovingly cured are now readily available at grocery stores—and not just fancy grocery stores either, but everyday supermarkets. You can put your own flavor stamp on them with this quick marinade. They'll keep absolutely forever in the fridge, and can be warmed in a matter of a few minutes for a no-hassle nibble.

MAKES 2½ CUPS

¼ cup olive oil (preferably Italian, for its spiciness)

3 tablespoons Caramelized Onion Compote (page 21)

Peel of ½ lemon, pith removed

Peel of ½ lime, pith removed

Peel of ½ orange, pith removed

¼ cup smoked almonds

1 ounce Fresno or other mild red chiles, sliced as thinly as possible

1 sprig each rosemary, thyme, and savory (if you can find it; sage if not), finely chopped

1 pound of your favorite mixed olives (such as kalamata, picholine, or castelvetrano)

1. In a medium saucepan set over low heat, heat the oil to 95°F. It should feel about body temperature, but use a thermometer to check it if possible.

2. Add the caramelized onion compote, citrus peels, smoked almonds, chiles, and herbs. Remove the oil from the heat and let the ingredients steep for 20 minutes. Add the olives and reheat it to 95°F. Strain off the oil and serve the olives warm. They can also be stored in the oil in the refrigerator for months.

SPICED ROASTED NUTS

When we were kids, my mum used to buy nuts still in the shell and give us a bowl and a cracker while we watched VHS tapes in front of the telly. The payoff was never rewarding enough for the amount of effort required to get the bloody thing out, so I spent most of my teens and twenties resenting nuts. But when I became the executive chef at a hotel called Palihouse in West Hollywood, the owners asked me to come up with snacks to put out in bowls at the bar. I wanted to do something sweet and salty, because every chef knows that's what makes people keep drinking; nuts were the obvious choice. Using my homemade spice mix set ours apart from the sort of thing you could buy in a shop. The result was good enough that it cured me of my nut aversion. Now these are a staple at my house for every barbecue and Premier League football game.

MAKES 3 CUPS

1 teaspoon chili powder

1 teaspoon paprika

1 teaspoon garam masala

½ cup confectioners' sugar

2 tablespoons kosher salt

½ cup shelled pistachios

½ cup shelled hazelnuts

½ cup shelled walnuts

½ cup cashews

½ cup shelled peanuts

½ cup macadamia nuts

1. Preheat the oven to 325°F.

2. In a small bowl, mix together the chili powder, paprika, garam masala, confectioners' sugar, and salt. In a large bowl, mix all the nuts.

3. Dust the spice mix over to the nuts and mix it up with your hands until things are evenly distributed. Spread the nuts in a single layer on a baking sheet and bake them for 20 minutes. Serve them once they've cooled. They keep for about a week in an airtight container.

WHIPPED LARDO

The word *lardo* gives the distinct impression of something that's going to give you an early heart attack, but the truth is that animal fats, when obtained from quality sources, aren't nearly as bad for us as we've made them out to be in recent years. My granddad lived until he was well into his nineties, and he subsisted on the likes of butter, lard, cheese, full-fat milk, and cream. So go ahead and enjoy your lardo as a tremendously tasty substitute for butter.

MAKES 1½ TO 2 CUPS

8 ounces top-quality pork fatback

½ cup coarse sea salt or kosher salt

1 garlic clove

1 teaspoon sherry vinegar

½ teaspoon kosher salt

½ teaspoon freshly ground black pepper

½ teaspoon finely chopped fresh rosemary

½ teaspoon finely chopped fresh thyme

Warm crusty bread for serving

Thinly shaved radishes for serving, optional

Handful of watercress for serving, optional

1. Sprinkle the fatback with the coarse sea salt and place it in a container in the fridge for 24 hours. This is a simple cure, meant to pull out excess water and amplify the fat's porky flavor.

2. Wash the pork under cold water for 2 minutes, then cut into ½-inch pieces.

3. Grate the garlic using a Microplane grater; alternatively, smash it, sprinkle it with kosher salt, and grind it to a paste using the back of your chef's knife. The latter method has the disadvantage of taking longer and making your cutting board smell permanently of garlic.

4. Chuck the fatback, garlic, vinegar, kosher salt, pepper, rosemary, and thyme into a food processor. Pulse the motor a few times to combine the ingredients, then process until smooth. Serve the lardo at room temperature with warm crusty bread and some shaved radish and/or watercress.

SRIRACHA DEVILED EGGS

Who doesn't love a deviled egg? These one-bite beauties are the perfect companions to a cold beer—better than your mum's, although don't tell her I said so. Bet you can't eat just six!

A word about the eggs: don't be a cheapskate. Buy the free-range organic eggs. Not only is it the right thing to do, but you'll be rewarded by the better-tasting yolks of chickens who aren't being tortured.

SERVES 4 TO 6

12 large organic eggs

¾ cup mayonnaise

½ teaspoon Thai
red curry paste

Zest and juice of 1 lime

Drizzle of Sriracha sauce,
plus more to taste

Drizzle of Tabasco sauce

1 teaspoon Thai fish sauce

1 teaspoon Dijon mustard

8 slices crisp bacon, broken
into 3 even pieces each

¼ cup chopped fresh chives
or green scallion tops

Salt

1. Place the eggs in a large pot and cover them by an inch with warm water. Bring the water to a boil over high heat and boil the eggs for 8 minutes—best to set a timer so that you don't end up with overcooked, powdery egg yolks. Transfer the eggs to a bowl of ice water to chill down.

2. Peel the eggs, gently cut them in half from top to bottom, and transfer the yolks to the bowl of a food processor. Add the mayo, curry paste, lime zest and juice, Sriracha, Tabasco, fish sauce, and mustard and blend until smooth, about 1 minute (this can also be done by hand, but the yolks won't be as creamy).

3. Taste the yolk mixture and add salt if needed. If it's not devilish enough for you, add some more Sriracha.

4. Scoop the yolk mixture into a piping bag and squeeze it into the cavity of each egg white. Pro tip: if you don't have a piping bag, you can cut the corner off a zip-top bag, seal the yolk mixture inside, and squeeze it out that way.

5. Poke a piece of bacon into each egg half and sprinkle with the chives or scallion tops. Pop open a beer and eat.

FRESH RICOTTA WITH CRUSTY BREAD

The first time you make this and don't fuck it up you'll be mighty impressed with yourself, and you're going to want all your mates around to see. But the truth is that making ricotta is dead easy, just as long as you get good-quality milk and don't scorch it by letting it get too hot. The straining process takes a little time, but you can put it off to the side and forget about it for half an hour.

MAKES 2 CUPS

6½ cups organic whole milk

1½ cups organic heavy cream

Kosher salt

1 tablespoon fresh lemon juice

2½ tablespoons distilled white vinegar

1 loaf crusty bread, such as a baguette

A little olive oil, sea salt, and freshly cracked pepper

1. Line a large sieve or strainer of some description with 2 layers of cheesecloth (or a coffee filter, in a pinch) and set it over a large, deep bowl.

2. Bring the milk, cream, and 1 teaspoon kosher salt to a simmer in a large stainless steel pot (don't use one made from a reactive metal like aluminum or copper, which will make the ricotta taste funny) over medium heat, stirring it occasionally. Add the lemon juice and vinegar and cook, stirring, until the mixture curdles, about 1 minute.

3. Pour the mixture into the prepared sieve and let it drain, discarding the liquid (called whey) from the bowl as necessary, for at least 15 minutes and up to 30 minutes. The longer it drains, the thicker the cheese.

4. Toast the bread; sprinkle the soft ricotta with sea salt and freshly cracked pepper, drizzle it with a good slick of olive oil, and serve warm.

PORK SCRATCHINGS

When I was a kid, pork scratchings—also known as pork rinds, or *chicharrónes* to the Spaniards—were something I often had when I went to the pub with my parents. A shandy and a packet of pork scratchings. Since then they've found their way into mainstream gourmet kitchens, where they're valued for their intensely crunchy texture and the funky look they have about them. Mostly I'm just crazy for the way they taste. You're unlikely to find pork skin at the A&P, but a local butcher should be more than happy to offload his excess to you for a few pennies a pound.

SERVES 8 TO 10

The skin from 1 pork belly (about 12 × 20 inches), trimmed of excess fat and nipples, if present

Kosher salt

Sunflower or vegetable oil for frying

Sea salt and freshly ground white pepper for seasoning

Applesauce or salsa for dipping

1. In a large pot, cover the pork skin by 2 inches of water as salty as seawater. Weigh the pork skin down with a plate to keep it submerged and bring the water to a boil. Boil, uncovered, until the water is white and the skin is soft and pliable but not falling apart, 1½ to 2 hours. Add more water as needed to keep the skin submerged; no need to watch it like a hawk the entire time, just check it from time to time to make sure the water doesn't boil dry.

2. Set a wire rack on top of a baking sheet and, using a slotted spoon, carefully transfer the pork skin to the rack in an even layer. Chuck it in the fridge, uncovered, and allow it to chill for at least an hour.

3. Preheat the oven to its lowest temperature setting—this should be 180 to 200°F, depending on your oven.

4. Once the skin is chilled, use a spoon or a bench scraper (or even a wallpaper scraper) to remove all the fat; you have to be somewhat careful here not to break the skin.

5. Line a baking sheet with parchment paper and place the skin in a single layer on top. Dry the skin in the oven until all the moisture has evaporated and it becomes brown and brittle. This should take about 6 hours, but start checking it after 4. If it's gone black, you know you fucked up and you had better call the butcher and get some more.

6. Snap the skin into small pieces about 1 inch square. I've used a Dremel in the past to create exactly uniform squares; I've also just snapped them with my fingers into uneven shapes. Either way works. At this stage, you can store the pieces in an airtight container in the cupboard for a couple of days before frying.

7. Take a heavy-bottomed pot, like a Dutch oven, and fill it half full with oil. Position a thermometer in the oil and heat it nice and slow over medium heat until the temperature reads between 385 and 400°F. It's important that the temperature stays within this range. Fry a couple of pieces of pork skin at a

time, prodding them until they puff up and turn crispy, about 15 seconds. Transfer them to a paper towel-lined tray and season them with salt and pepper while still hot. Repeat with the remaining pieces. Serve immediately with applesauce or salsa, or cool them to room temperature and store them in an airtight container for up to 2 weeks.

BAGNA CAUDA WITH MARKET VEGETABLES

I grew up eating good but simple English food, so when I moved to London and was exposed to the diversity of cuisines there, my taste buds went into shock. I remember so well my first Caesar salad—exotic fare for a kid from Nottingham—and how surprised I was to discover that gloriously rich dressing got its meaty flavor from anchovies. As it turns out, those nasty-looking little fillets are at the heart of many great dressings and sauces, including this one.

Bagna cauda simply means "hot dip" in Italian, and it's a creamy, mildly fishy, fondue-like sauce that pairs particularly well with fresh vegetables. Needless to say, it will be a major upgrade from that seven-layer dip you've been serving since college.

SERVES 6

½ cup plus 2 tablespoons extra-virgin olive oil

4 to 5 garlic cloves, peeled and grated on a Microplane

12 anchovies preserved in olive oil, drained and minced

¼ cup whole milk

6 to 8 tablespoons unsalted butter, cut into chunks

Various raw farmers' market vegetables, such as fennel, cauliflower, Belgian endive, sweet bell peppers, and zucchini

1. In a small saucepan over low heat, combine the oil, garlic, and anchovies and whisk them constantly for 3 to 4 minutes. The anchovies will break apart and disperse in the oil. Whisk in the milk, followed by 6 tablespoons cold butter. As soon as the butter has melted, remove the sauce from the heat and give it a few more beats with your whisk so that everything is creamy and emulsified.

2. Taste the dip; if it's a bit too fishy for you, add 2 tablespoons more butter. Just remember that you'll be eating it in small amounts to liven up plain vegetables, so it should have a powerful flavor.

3. Wash the veggies and chop them into pieces appropriate for dipping. Serve with the warm dip.

FRIED SQUASH BLOSSOMS

I love spring and summer, and it's not because I pull out the Bermuda shorts and SPF 100 and hit the beach. I'm always at work. It's because of the quality and freshness of the fruits and veggies at the farmers' market. In the spring you have peas, morels, asparagus—everything green—and then through the summer, all the colors: stone fruits, berries, peppers, eggplant, sweet corn, and tomatoes. Nestled in between all that are squash blossoms, which are the edible flowers of zucchini plants. You'll find those at farmers' markets from May to September. Some chefs like to fill and steam them, but for me, the best way is fried crispy in beer batter, oozing with hot goat cheese, and dipped in chili marmalade.

SERVES 4 TO 6

1 cup creamy goat cheese

¼ cup grated Parmesan

1 large egg yolk

1 teaspoon chopped fresh basil

Pinch of freshly grated nutmeg (less is more here)

Pinch of cayenne pepper (ditto)

Kosher salt and freshly ground black pepper

12 large squash blossoms

2 cups lukewarm light beer

1 teaspoon active dry yeast

¼ cup vodka

1 cup Wondra flour, plus more for dredging

2 large egg whites

4 to 5 ice cubes

Sunflower or vegetable oil for frying

Sweet Chili Marmalade for dipping (page 26)

1. In a small bowl, mix together the goat cheese, Parmesan, egg yolk, basil, nutmeg, cayenne, and a bit of salt and pepper and stir until smooth. Spoon the filling into a heavy-duty 1-quart plastic bag, squeeze out the air, and seal it. Snip one of the corners off the bag to create a small hole. Gently insert the cut corner all the way to the bottom of a squash blossom and pipe about a tablespoon of the goat cheese filling inside. Twist the top of the flower closed, making sure to completely seal in the filling so that it won't tumble out. Repeat with the remaining squash blossoms and bang them in the fridge until the cheese is set, at least 30 minutes.

2. In a really large bowl, combine the beer, yeast, and vodka, then whisk in the flour until smooth. Whisk the egg whites to soft peaks in a separate bowl, then gently fold them into the beer mixture. Drop in the ice cubes and let it sit covered with a tea towel somewhere warm until doubled or tripled in size, about 20 minutes.

3. Now we're going to make a deep-fryer. If you've got an electric one by chance, use it, because they're way safer; if not, take a heavy pot like a Dutch oven and fill it half full with cooking oil. Position a thermometer in the oil and heat it nice and slow over medium heat until the temperature reads 350°F. Drop a bit of batter carefully into the oil; it should sizzle immediately. This setup will work for anything you want to deep-fry, not just squash blossoms.

4. Remove the blossoms from the refrigerator and dredge them in flour on all sides. Shake off the excess flour and dip them into the beer batter. Let the excess batter drip off.

5. Gently lay the squash blossoms in the hot oil. Don't just lob them in, lads; I can't stress how stupid and dangerous that would be, as you don't want to be putting out a grease fire, ever. Working with about 6 blossoms at a time, fry them until pale golden brown, 2 to 3 minutes. Use a metal spoon to flip them over from time to time so that they cook evenly. Remove them from the oil with a slotted spoon and let them cool off slightly. Serve them with sweet chili marmalade for dipping.

GOUGÈRES

These fancy little cheese puffs are the original "once you pop, you just can't stop" finger food. By some kind of Frenchie magic, they pack tons of toasted cheese flavor into a light, airy little ball. Gougères can be a bit tricky to make, so read the recipe all the way through before you start.

MAKES 15 TO 20

½ cup water

½ cup whole milk

½ cup (1 stick) unsalted butter, cut into small cubes

Large pinch of kosher salt

1 cup all-purpose flour

4 large eggs

1 cup (3½ ounces) finely shredded Gruyère, plus more for sprinkling

¼ teaspoon freshly ground black pepper

Small pinch of freshly grated nutmeg

1. Preheat the oven to 400°F. Line 2 baking sheets with parchment paper, or if you're the sort to have silicone baking mats around the house, those are even better. Set the baking sheets aside.

2. In a medium saucepan, combine the water, milk, butter, and salt and bring to a boil. Add the flour and stir it with a wooden spoon until a smooth dough forms. Turn the heat to low and continue stirring vigorously until the dough dries out and pulls away from the pan, about 2 minutes. If you have a stand mixer, plug that baby in.

3. Scrape the dough into the bowl of the stand mixer and let it cool for 1 minute. Fit the mixer with the paddle attachment, turn the machine to medium speed, and add the eggs one at a time—and I do mean one at a time, chaps—beating them in thoroughly between each addition. Add the cheese and a pinch each of pepper and nutmeg, then mix for a minute more. All this can also be done by hand, tedious as it may be.

4. Get out a pastry bag; if you don't have a pastry bag, jerry-rig one by cutting the corner off a 1-gallon zip-top bag. Now fit the bag with a ½-inch round tip—this one we can't get around, so you'll have to go and purchase a pastry tip if you don't already have one (remember how I said to read the recipe first?). Fill the pastry bag with dough and pipe tablespoon-sized mounds onto the baking sheets a couple of inches apart.

5. Sprinkle the dough with cheese and bake for 22 minutes, or until puffed and golden brown. Serve hot, or cool them to room temperature, freeze them in a zip-top bag, and reheat them in a preheated 350°F oven until piping hot.

PIGS IN BLANKETS

A simple recipe like this one is all about buying some good-quality ingredients and then filling the house up with wicked aromas ASAP. I could give you a hundred different sausage recipes that you probably would never even read, and the truth is that most professional kitchens don't even make their own puff pastry anymore. So why fuck about wasting everyone's time? Let's make it easy, bake it fresh, and make it yours.

SERVES 6

2 tablespoons extra-virgin olive oil

1 onion, finely chopped

1 tablespoon chopped fresh sage

6 (4-ounce) fresh pork sausages (never frozen!)

Handful of dried bread crumbs

Tiny pinch of freshly grated nutmeg

4 sheets ready-made puff pastry

1 large organic egg

A bit of milk

1. Preheat the oven to 350°F and cover a baking sheet with parchment paper.

2. Heat the oil in a medium saucepan over medium heat and add the onion. Cook until soft and golden brown, about 5 minutes. Add the sage and cook for a couple of minutes more, then spread the mixture out onto a plate or baking sheet to cool off.

3. Using a sharp knife, slit the skins of the sausages and pop the meat out into a large bowl along with the cooled sage and onion mixture, the bread crumbs, and nutmeg. Mix well with your (preferably clean) hands until all is evenly combined.

4. Hopefully your puff pastry came ready-sheeted; if not, on a floured work surface, roll the pastry out to form four 8 × 10-inch rectangles about 1/8 inch thick. Cut each lengthwise into 2 even rectangles about 4 inches wide. Now roll the sausage mixture into 8 long tubes and place each in the center of a piece of pastry dough.

5. Create an egg wash by whisking together the egg and milk. Brush the exposed surfaces of the pastry with the egg wash, then fold it up to wrap the sausage inside. Press down gently to seal.

6. Cut the long sausage rolls into the sizes you want (bigger is not always better, Yanks) and space them out on the baking sheet. Brush the rolls with the rest of the egg wash and bake them in the oven for about 20 minutes, until golden brown and cooked through. Serve hot, ideally with Walnut Mustard (page 29) and, to make a meal of it, Butter Lettuce Salad (page 121).

FISHES

WHEN I WAS A CHILD I HATED FISH, AND I ALWAYS KNEW WHEN WE WERE HAVING
it for dinner because I could smell it all the way from the garden. To this day I have issues
with salmon, because my granny would cook the life out of it and mash it, skin, bones,
and all, into a sandwich filling. I get the sense that a lot of people are still recovering
from their own fish phobias instilled by horrible childhood eating experiences (sorry,
mums) and need to be coaxed back into buying and cooking our finned friends.

What is it about fish that intimidates people so? I've seen grown men cower in
front of the seafood counter, utterly confused by what to buy and how on earth they'll
cook it once they get it home. This is a shame, because even with all the concerns today
about sustainability and overfishing, seafood remains one of the best things you can
feed yourself. It's delicious, good for you, and carries a much smaller environmental
impact than land meats like beef and pork. We should all be eating more fish, full stop.

Most people avoid cooking fish at home because they're worried that they're
going to mess it up: undercook it, overcook it, or break it to mush in the pan. In this
chapter, I provide a series of dead simple methods for preparing all types of seafood.
Once you've mastered these techniques—from milk poaching, to baking, to pan roasting—
you'll be able to handle pretty much anything the seafood counter can throw at you.

WHOLE FISH IN FOIL

This recipe deserves a place on the greatest hits album without a doubt. It's very straightforward, hard to ruin with overcooking (everybody's worst fish cookery fear), and won't make your house smell like low tide. It also leaves you with a natural fish stock that can quickly be made into a butter sauce, making it mega-efficient for about fifteen minutes of prep time. It works for any whole fish small enough to fit inside a sheet of aluminum foil or parchment paper.

SERVES 2

1 (2½-pound) snapper or bass, scaled and gutted (look for fish with bright, wet eyes and pink gills)

Kosher salt

A good drizzle of extra-virgin olive oil

1 lemon, thinly sliced

1 large shallot, chopped

2 fresh bay leaves (dried can be substituted)

1 bundle assorted fresh herbs, such as thyme, rosemary, tarragon, and parsley, plus some extra to bed the fish on while cooking

4 garlic cloves, crushed with the back of a knife

2 cups good-quality dry white wine, plus extra for drinking

6 tablespoons unsalted cold butter, diced

Freshly ground black pepper

Fresh lemon juice

1. Preheat the oven to 400°F.

2. With a sharp knife, cut 3 diagonal incisions about ½-inch deep into both sides of the fish. Season the fish generously with salt all over and drizzle with oil inside and out. Place a few lemon slices, the shallot, bay leaves, bundle of mixed herbs, and 2 of the garlic cloves inside the fish.

3. Lay out a large piece of aluminum foil or parchment paper on top of a baking sheet, and in the center make a bed of the remaining herbs, lemon slices, and garlic. Place the fish on top. Gather the aluminum foil or parchment paper above the fish, folding it together to make a packet but leaving a small opening. Add the wine, then seal the foil completely.

4. Roast until the fish is just cooked through, 30 to 35 minutes. Remove it from the oven, open one end of the foil, and carefully (with a capital C!) pour off the liquid into a small saucepan. Bring it to a boil over high heat and reduce it by one third, 5 to 10 minutes. Turn the heat down to a slow simmer and whisk in the cold butter. Adjust the seasoning with salt, pepper, and a drop or two of lemon juice.

5. To fillet the fish, insert your knife just below the fish's head and run it along the spine toward the tail, lifting off the top fillet. Now grab hold of the tail and carefully lift the spine and ribs off the bottom fillet. For an extra flourish, fillet the big boy tableside. By the way, this is how you butcher any round fish, from trout to bass to cod, pike, snapper, and salmon.

6. Douse with your delicious pan sauce and serve.

FISH AND CHIPS

As a British chef, I've spent the past decade trying to avoid being reduced and pigeonholed to a fish and chips fry cook. I've filled my menus with the likes of hand-cut pastas, house-made charcuterie, and delicate, Japanese-style crudos, relegating the fish fry to the specials board. Just when I thought I had escaped the stereotype, I stopped making fish and chips altogether and was graciously but thoroughly reamed by my restaurant guests. So, in the interest of keeping everyone happy, here's my recipe. It's a good one. Expect gratitude for making it once and abuse if you don't make it again. Don't say I didn't warn you.

SERVES 4

2 teaspoons active dry yeast

1 cup warm water

¼ teaspoon paprika

¼ teaspoon ground turmeric

2 cups beer, plus more for drinking

2 teaspoons malt vinegar

1 cup all-purpose flour, plus more for dredging

1 cup cornstarch

Salt

1 large egg white, whisked to medium peaks

4 (6-ounce) pieces fresh cod, haddock, or halibut

Canola oil for frying

Triple-Cooked Chips (page 141)

Tartar Sauce (recipe opposite)

1 lemon, quartered

1. Make the batter: Activate the yeast by mixing it with warm water in a small bowl. Let it sit for a couple of minutes to start working, then add the paprika and turmeric. In a medium bowl, combine the beer and vinegar, then slowly whisk in the flour and cornstarch. Once the yeast mixture is bubbly, add it to the batter. Season the batter with a generous pinch of salt, then fold in the whipped egg white.

2. Now we're going to make a deep-fryer. If you've got an electric one by chance, use it, because they're way safer; if not, take a heavy-bottomed pot like a Dutch oven and fill it half full with oil. Position a thermometer in the oil and heat it nice and slow over medium heat until the temperature reads 350°F. Drop a bit of batter carefully into the oil; it should sizzle immediately.

3. Standing over your fryer, dip a piece of cod in the batter twice, ensuring that the entire fish is well-coated. If you have a fryer basket, use it; lay the fish gently into the oil and lift the fryer basket up, giving it a gentle shake to prevent the fish from settling on the bottom. If you don't have a fryer basket, lay the fish on a slotted spoon and lower it gently just below the surface of the oil, allowing the batter to crisp for 30 seconds or so before carefully removing the spoon. We're trying to keep the fish from dropping immediately to the bottom of the pot, where it will stick and fall apart if the batter hasn't crisped yet. Cook the fish for 4 to 5 minutes, until deep golden. Transfer it to a paper towel and repeat the process with the remaining fish.

4. While the fish is resting, fry your chips for their second time; transfer them to paper towels and hit them with a generous sprinkle of salt. Divide the fish and chips among 4 plates and serve them with a bowl of tartar sauce and lemon quarters.

TARTAR SAUCE

MAKES 1¾ CUPS

¾ cup mayonnaise

¼ small yellow onion, finely diced

2 tablespoons super-fine capers, rinsed
(minced regular capers can be substituted)

6 caper berries, stemmed and diced (these
are larger than capers, and with stems)

½ cup finely diced cornichons

2 tablespoons chopped fresh chives

2 tablespoons chopped fresh flat-leaf parsley

Mix everything together in a small bowl.

THE POWER OF THE BRINE

Brining fish may sound just a bit redundant—this is an animal that spent its whole life swimming around in brine, after all—but it's my secret weapon for fish cookery. Soaking fish in a saltwater solution firms up its flesh and seasons it throughout, extracting excess water and leaving just a pure flavor of fish behind. Brining allows the fillets or steaks to get really crisp when baked or sautéed, because they sear against the hot pan instead of steaming in their own juices.

To make a brine suitable for any and all fish, mix together a solution that's one fifth salt and four fifths water, plus a big pinch of sugar. Add aromatics that work well with fish, such as lemon zest, parsley, and thyme. Heat the liquid just to dissolve the salt and sugar, then chill it in the fridge until cold. Brine your fish for 35 minutes, rinse it, then let it dry out in the fridge between paper towels for at least 25 minutes. The surface of the fish should be dry to the touch. Now it's ready to cook; no additional seasoning necessary.

BAKED HALIBUT

America just loves halibut, probably because, like tuna, it tastes a bit like meat; it's one of the least "fishy" fish in the ocean. During Alaskan halibut season, which runs from May to September, I cook with it nonstop. This recipe also works for cod, flounder, sole—any skinless white fish. Just don't ever, ever buy tilapia. It tastes like garbage and is, for the most part, raised in squalor in Chinese fish farms.

One of the best ways to cook lean, flaky white fish is in a low oven, which cooks it through gently without drying out—as well as avoiding the sad fate of falling to shreds in a skillet. Use a toothpick or cake tester to tell when thicker fillets of fish are cooked through: when you think the fish is done, stab it with the toothpick. If it meets with resistance, the fish is still raw in the middle. If it moves through the flesh easily, you're in good shape.

SERVES 4

2 tablespoons chopped fresh chives

1 teaspoon lemon zest

1 tablespoon finely diced fresh ginger

4 tablespoons olive oil

4 (6-ounce) halibut fillets, each about 1½ inches thick

1 teaspoon kosher salt

¾ teaspoon freshly ground black pepper

Lemon wedges for garnish, optional

1. Preheat the oven to 325°F.

2. Make the topping: Mix the chives, lemon zest, ginger, and 2 tablespoons of the oil in a small bowl. Cover and chill. This can be prepared 4 hours ahead, but keep it cold.

3. Place the fillets on a baking sheet and coat them all over with the remaining 2 tablespoons oil. Sprinkle the tops of the fillets with salt, pepper, and the chive-lemon topping, giving it a good press so that it sticks. Bake the fish just until cooked through, 9 to 10 minutes. Serve immediately with lemon wedges.

MILK-POACHED SMOKED SALMON

This dish has a vaguely trendy feel to it, owing to the Nordic fondness for smoked fish and for whey poaching: a technique for slowly cooking meats and fishes in the tangy liquid by-product of cheese making. The difference is that I use milk instead of whey, and I've been poaching smoked salmon in it since Rene Redzepi was still reading comic books under his bed.

Notice that we're using hot-smoked, or "kippered" salmon in this recipe. So, not the cold-smoked, translucent, thinly sliced stuff that you get in vacuum packs at the grocery store and put on top of bagels. Hot-smoked salmon is meaty, opaque, flaky, and sold in fillets. It's less common than the cold-smoked variety, so you're going to have to go somewhere with a decent smoked fish selection to find it.

SERVES 4

4 cups whole milk

½ cup water

Some parsley stalks (minus the leaves)

1 bay leaf

4 (6-ounce) skin-on hot-smoked salmon portions

6 ounces Herb Butter (page 35)

1 bag prewashed spinach leaves

Kosher salt and freshly ground black pepper

1. Find a pan about 4 inches deep and big enough in diameter to comfortably hold the salmon portions. Add the milk and water, a few parsley stalks, and the bay leaf. Bring it to a boil over high heat; the water should stop the milk from scorching. Turn the heat down to a gentle simmer and add the salmon.

2. Poach the salmon for 5 minutes, or until it's cooked to a medium temperature throughout. The salmon should retain some pinkness, and the skin should peel off with a gentle pull. Transfer it to a paper towel-lined plate and allow the excess milk to drain off. Place a small pat of herb butter on top of each fillet and allow it to melt.

3. In a large sauté pan over medium-low heat, melt the remaining herb butter. Once it begins to foam, add the spinach and sauté it until wilted. Season with salt and pepper.

4. Divide the spinach among 4 plates and top with the salmon fillets.

ROASTED OYSTERS WITH CURRIED APPLE BUTTER

Raw oysters tend to be a "love it or hate it" food, and personally, I've never been a huge fan. I struggle to understand why people don't cook them more often. Broiled with a knob of spiced butter on top, their flesh firms up and caramelizes as it roasts. That signature, briny flavor is balanced out by the richness of the butter. What's not to like?

SERVES 4 TO 6

½ cup (1 stick) unsalted butter, softened

½ teaspoon Madras curry powder

¼ teaspoon smoked Spanish paprika

¼ teaspoon cayenne pepper

1 tablespoon chopped fresh cilantro

2 tablespoons peeled, finely diced apple, preferably Granny Smith

A squeeze of lemon juice, dash of kosher salt, and grind of black pepper

1 dozen large oysters, such as Barnstable, Hama Hama, or Blue Point

Sea salt

1. In a medium bowl, combine the butter, curry powder, paprika, cayenne, cilantro, apple, lemon juice, salt, and pepper and mix them up with a spatula or wooden spoon until evenly combined.

2. Heat your broiler or grill for medium-high-heat cooking. Crack open the oysters and discard the top halves of each shell. Detach the oysters from their bottom shells and turn the meat upside down so that the plump side faces up. Set them on a baking sheet atop little mounds of sea salt, which will keep them from tipping over.

3. Spoon a level teaspoon of the butter mixture on top of each oyster. Place them under the broiler or on the grill and cook them for 3 to 4 minutes, until the butter is melted and begins to caramelize.

4. Crack open a beer and scarf them down hot.

OYSTERS 101

If you're gearing up to shuck oysters at home, there's likely just one question at the top of your mind: how will I know if I get a bad one?

Trust me, you'll know. The oyster will feel light for its size. The shell might be brittle and flaky. There will be a lack of liquor inside, or what's there will look milky rather than clear. The oyster itself will be dry and wrinkled. The smell will be off; fishy, not fresh and sweet. And if by some chance you still decide to try the bloody thing, it will taste metallic and rancid. But really, don't try it.

The best way to avoid bad oysters has to do with how you buy them. Getting them shipped direct from the oyster farm is ideal, as you know they'll be just two to three days out of the water. If you're picking them up at a seafood counter, you want to know their harvest date. The law requires shops to keep a slip that says where oysters were harvested and when, and if you've got an honest supplier, they'll be happy to show it to you. Avoid anything that's been out of the water for a week or more.

Once you get your oysters home, store them cup-side down in as cold a place as possible. If your fridge isn't 35°F or below, chuck some ice on top of them to help chill them down. Don't ever put oysters in the freezer, though. They need to be kept alive until you eat them.

The fastest way to open a small oyster is to stick the tip of a paring knife right into the hinge and twist it to open the shell. A dull-tipped oyster knife is definitely the safer alternative, and therefore I'll make that my official recommendation. No matter what you use and what sort of oyster you're opening, be sure to wedge the knife as deeply into the oyster's hinge as possible before you start prying it open. Smaller oysters tend to be easier to open, but this isn't always the case.

There are loads of oyster varieties out there, and whether you want Wellfleets, Blue Points, Kumamotos, Olde Salts, Beau Soleils, or any other kind all comes down to personal preference. There's no "best" variety. Oysters differ in flavor and texture based on the species as well as where they grow. In general, the cold water of the east coast tends to produce firmer, meatier, and saltier specimens, with west coast oysters being creamier and sweeter.

PAN-ROASTED SALMON

The number one mistake that people make when cooking fish on the stovetop is—gather round close, now—not letting the pan get hot enough before adding the fish. If that metal isn't really, properly blazing hot, the fish will stick to it and proceed to fall apart when you try to flip it (sound familiar?). So go on, throw open a window, turn the venting on high, take the battery out of your smoke detector if you dare, and wait for the oil to shimmer and smoke before you move a muscle.

Equipment is also key. Use a pan with a nonstick surface: cast iron, black steel, or Teflon all work. An easy rule of thumb is to pick a pan with a dark cooking surface. Aluminum or stainless steel won't do. Finally, be sure to leave the fish alone until it releases from the pan on its own, rather than trying to scrape it up and flip it just because the timer's gone off.

Follow these three guidelines and you have a fighting chance of not fucking up.

SERVES 4

2 tablespoons grapeseed or vegetable oil

4 (6-ounce) skin-on center-cut salmon fillets

Kosher salt

Freshly ground black pepper

½ lemon

1. Preheat the oven to 350°F.

2. Heat the oil in a large, ovenproof cast-iron, black steel, or Teflon skillet over medium-high heat. Dry off the salmon fillets between paper towels and season them with salt (never add pepper at this stage; pepper burns).

3. Once the pan is piping hot and the oil has begun to smoke, add the salmon skin-side down. Press gently on the fillets with a spatula to ensure that the skin is in full contact with the pan and cook without touching it until the skin is golden and crisp, about 5 minutes.

4. Transfer the pan to the oven and roast the salmon until opaque, 4 to 5 minutes. The exact timing will depend on the thickness of the fillets; it should measure 125°F in the center. Remove it from the oven, quickly turn over the salmon, and spoon the cooking oil over the top a couple of times. Divide the fillets among 4 plates. Season with a little salt, a grind of pepper, and a squeeze of lemon and serve.

SMOKED SALMON AND POTATO TERRINE WITH SAUCE GRIBICHE

This terrine is a pain in the bollocks to make. It takes time, skill, and a good amount of patience. But it's delicious and looks spectacular as an appetizer, brunch dish, or part of a truly impressive charcuterie board. What can I say; cooking needn't always be about what's quick and sensible. So, man up! Get your tape measure out and start laying down salmon and potatoes.

MAKES ONE 8 × 4-INCH TERRINE

4 large Yukon gold potatoes or other large waxy potatoes

Salt

½ full side sliced smoked salmon (I really like Scottish salmon)

Anchovy Butter (recipe opposite)

Sauce Gribiche (recipe opposite)

1. Peel the potatoes and slice them paper-thin, about $1/16$-inch thick. If you have a little meat slicer or a mandoline (the slicer, not the mini guitar), this is a good time to dust it off and use it. Watch your fingers.

2. Fill a large saucepan two thirds full with salted water and bring it to a boil. Add the sliced potatoes and simmer until soft but not falling apart, 15 to 20 minutes. Remove the pot from the heat and allow the potatoes to cool in the water to room temperature, about 30 minutes (this part is important; if you drain them while hot, they'll fall to pieces). Remove the potatoes from the water with a slotted spoon and dry them using paper towels.

3. Line a terrine mold or loaf pan about 8 × 4 inches in size with plastic wrap, leaving enough of an overhang on all sides to completely cover the top of the terrine when folded. Now line the bottom and inside walls of the terrine with the largest pieces of smoked salmon, covering all five sides without allowing the pieces to overlap. Brush the bottom with anchovy butter.

4. Your potatoes should now be dry, and here's where the tape measure comes in: you need to cover the bottom of the terrine perfectly with potato slices that have been measured and trimmed appropriately, like building a stone wall—no gaps or overlaps. Then brush the potatoes with anchovy butter. Cover the potatoes with a single layer of smoked salmon and brush it with anchovy butter. Repeat with the remaining potatoes and smoked salmon until the terrine is full to the brim, finishing with a layer of salmon on top. My best time for this is 18 minutes, so add an hour on to that and you should be good.

5. Fold any overhanging salmon over the top of the terrine, followed by the plastic wrap. Wrap the whole terrine in a few more layers of plastic wrap until it's very tightly sealed, then press down on it as hard as you can to force any air out (you can also put it on the floor and stand on it—just don't fall over). Refrigerate the terrine for at least 2 hours and up to a week.

6. Remove the terrine from its mold and rewrap it tightly in fresh plastic wrap to help it hold its shape when sliced (it's a bit fragile, so a really sharp knife will come in handy). Cut it into ½-inch slices, and make sure you have plenty of mates around to show off to. Serve with a bowl of sauce gribiche on the side.

ANCHOVY BUTTER
MAKES 1 CUP

1 cup (2 sticks) unsalted butter
3 to 4 anchovy fillets
1 tablespoon chopped fresh parsley

1. Place the butter in a microwave-safe bowl. Heat it for 10 seconds at a time in the microwave until it liquefies but the butterfat has not separated from the butter solids.

2. Mince the anchovies to a fine paste, then add them along with the parsley into the liquefied butter and whisk until evenly combined.

SAUCE GRIBICHE
MAKES 1 CUP

2 tablespoons finely chopped cornichons or small pickles
2 tablespoons finely chopped capers
½ teaspoon chopped fresh parsley
½ teaspoon chopped fresh tarragon
½ teaspoon chopped fresh chives
½ teaspoon chopped fresh chervil
½ cup mayonnaise
1 egg, hard-boiled and chopped

In a medium bowl, mix all the ingredients until well-combined. This sauce can be made a day in advance and stored in the refrigerator.

SALMON ON A CEDAR PLANK

I've written three different salmon recipes into this book, and it's not because salmon is my favorite fish. But it's incredibly popular and widely available in the States these days, so I figure you ought to have a few good ways to cook it in your back pocket. This easy cedar plank method keeps the fish from drying out and flavors it gently with the warm scent of cedar. If you don't fancy grilling, it can just as easily be done in a 300°F oven.

SERVES 4

Kosher salt

4 (6- to 8-ounce) salmon fillets

Freshly ground black pepper

6 tablespoons Dijon mustard

6 tablespoons maple sugar (brown sugar may be substituted)

1 lemon, cut in half

1. Soak a cedar plank about 6 × 14 inches in size in lightly salted water for 2 hours. Drain.

2. Remove the skin from each salmon fillet and season both sides well with salt and pepper. Place the fillets on the cedar plank and brush the tops and sides liberally with mustard. Sprinkle them evenly with the maple sugar.

3. Prepare your grill for indirect heat cooking; for a gas grill, this means lighting only half of it, and for a charcoal grill it means banking the coals to one side. While the grill is heating, place the salmon and plank on the side of the grill away from the flame and drop the cover of the grill. The temperature should be around 300°F. Cook the fish for 15 to 20 minutes; the internal temperature of the salmon should read 125°F for medium rare, which is how I like it. If you want it medium-well, leave it for another 5 to 10 minutes.

4. Remove the fish from the grill and squeeze lemon juice over the fillets. Serve them right off the plank, with potatoes and salad.

QUINOA AND SHELLFISH PAELLA

Each summer growing up, the Collinses had our two weeks somewhere warm in mainland Europe to get sunburned and sleep late. One year, on a trip to the island of Majorca, my mum was adamant that we experience the local culture. I immediately took to Spanish food—it's hard not to like crispy-fried *patatas bravas*, oozing *croquetas*, and Serrano ham, after all—but wasn't so sure about the paella. Rice was still a novelty in 1980s Britain, and it wasn't for me. Years later, when I moved to the States and discovered quinoa, I knew that it would make a perfect substitute. It might fly in the face of tradition, but I find quinoa easier to eat than rice and really dig how it absorbs all the dish's delicious flavors while adding a pleasing crunch.

SERVES 4

1 tablespoon extra-virgin olive oil

1 large onion, diced

1 carrot, diced

1 rib celery, diced

1 leek, diced

4 piquillo peppers, diced

2 medium tomatoes, diced

2 garlic cloves, minced

4 ounces Spanish chorizo, diced

1 cup quinoa, rinsed

1 teaspoon curry powder

¼ teaspoon Spanish paprika

1 cup white wine

1 (8-ounce) bottle clam juice

4 ounces raw jumbo shrimp, peeled and deveined

6 ounces clams

6 ounces mussels

4 ounces cooked lobster meat, chopped

4 ounces fresh scallops

2 tablespoons chopped fresh flat-leaf parsley

1 teaspoon chopped fresh dill

2 tablespoons chopped fresh cilantro

Salt and black pepper

1 tablespoon fresh lemon juice

1. In a Dutch oven over medium-high heat, heat the oil until it shimmers. Chuck in the diced vegetables and cook for 5 minutes, or until they're soft and beginning to color. Add the garlic, chorizo, quinoa, and spices and cook for another 5 minutes.

2. Stir in the wine and let it reduce by half. Add the clam juice, cover the pot with a lid, reduce the heat, and let it slowly simmer for about 15 minutes.

3. Now add the shrimp and stir them around for 30 seconds, or until they begin to turn pink. Add the clams and mussels, cover the pot, and cook for about 4 minutes, until the shells open.

4. Stir the lobster and scallops into the quinoa; you're basically just warming them through and lightly cooking the scallops. Stir in the chopped fresh herbs and season the dish with salt, pepper, and the lemon juice. Drizzle a little bit of oil over the top, place the pot in the middle of the table, and serve.

SQUID INK CAPPELLINI WITH LOBSTER BOLOGNESE

This dish has been on my menus for years, and during that time has developed a solid fan following. In the restaurant, we make a rich stock from lobster shells and use that as the basis for the Bolognese sauce; for the home cook, you can save yourself a lot of hard work by buying a jar of concentrated "lobster base," which reconstitutes in hot water into stock (hey, I won't tell if you won't . . .). If you're not up to making the squid ink pasta, any regular store-bought cappellini will do. Truth be told, though, the squid ink pasta really makes the dish for me, so why not borrow a pasta machine and give it a go? Either way, it's rock star pasta, and a very solid move for date night with the missus.

SERVES 4 TO 6

4 tablespoons vegetable oil

1½ cups sliced or diced white mushrooms

1 small carrot, finely chopped

½ onion, finely chopped

3 ribs celery, finely chopped

1 leek, white part only, finely chopped

4 garlic cloves, finely chopped

Kosher salt

1½ tablespoons lobster base

1 tablespoon tomato paste

2 cups white wine

4 cups canned chopped tomatoes, preferably San Marzano tomatoes from Italy

12 tablespoons (1½ sticks) unsalted butter

Squid Ink Cappellini (recipe follows) or store-bought cappellini

10 to 12 ounces cooked lobster tail meat, diced

A squeeze of lemon juice

1. Heat 1 tablespoon of the oil in a medium sauté pan set over medium-high heat. Once the oil is shimmering, add the mushrooms and cook, stirring occasionally, until soft and golden brown, 5 to 7 minutes. Set them aside.

2. Heat the remaining 3 tablespoons oil in a 5- or 6-quart pot over medium heat. Add the carrots, onion, celery, leek, and garlic to the pot and season with a large pinch of salt. Sweat the vegetables slowly, letting them release their juices without coloring, 2 to 3 minutes.

3. Stir in the lobster base and tomato paste and cook for 3 minutes. Add the wine and scrape the browned bits off the surface of the pan while it bubbles (this is called *deglazing*). Reduce the wine until nearly dry, 5 to 10 minutes, then add the tomatoes.

4. Simmer the sauce slowly over medium-low heat for 30 to 45 minutes, stirring it frequently to ensure that it doesn't stick to the bottom of the pan and burn. Remove it from the heat and stir through the butter.

5. Meanwhile, bring 4 quarts of seawater-salty water to a boil. Drop the fresh pasta in and cook it for 2 minutes. Lift the pasta from the water with tongs, transfer it to the tomato sauce, and cook it for a further 30 to 45 seconds. Add the cooked mushrooms and lobster meat and cook for 1 minute, just to heat the lobster through. Taste and add salt as needed. Using tongs, lift the pasta from the pan into bowls. Squeeze a bit of lemon juice over the top and serve.

SQUID INK CAPPELLINI

MAKES 1 POUND

1¼ cups tipo "00" flour

Pinch of salt

2 large whole eggs

3 large egg yolks

½ teaspoon olive oil

½ tablespoon squid ink

Semolina flour, optional

1. Combine the flour and salt in food processor. Crack the eggs and yolks into a small cup and whisk in the oil and squid ink. With the food processor running, add the egg mixture to the flour in a quick stream. Give the machine a good shake to bring everything together to form a loose, crumbly dough. Dump it all out onto a work surface and, using your hands, press the dough into a shaggy single mass.

2. Start to knead the dough with your right hand by folding the back edge toward you, and then pushing it down and away with the heel of your hand. Turn the dough a quarter turn and repeat for 5 to 10 minutes. You'll know the dough has been kneaded properly when it has formed into a smooth, elastic mass and bounces back when you press it with your finger.

3. Wrap the dough in plastic wrap and place it in the refrigerator to rest for at least 30 minutes but ideally overnight.

4. Dust a baking sheet with flour, preferably semolina flour, or if not, Tipo "00" flour. Roll the dough out using a pasta machine fitted with a cappellini attachment according to the manufacturer's instructions. Lay the strands of pasta flat on the sheet, dust them with flour, and let them sit at room temperature until you're ready to use them.

Note: If you don't have food processor, you can make pasta dough using what is known as the "well" method. Mix the flour and salt together on a work surface and create a well in the center of the flour. Add the egg mixture and, working from the inner edges of the well outward, use a fork to slowly incorporate the flour into the liquid until everything is combined into a shaggy dough. Knead the dough as instructed above to produce your smooth elastic ball, wrap, and place in the refrigerator to rest.

OCTOPUS SALAD

Congratulations! If you're reading this, it means you saw the word *octopus* and didn't immediately turn the page. Thanks for bearing with me.

In the wrong hands, octopus can be tough, rubbery, and bland, but trust me that this Mediterranean-style salad is packed with flavor and not very difficult to pull off. In fact, the hardest part of this recipe will be finding somewhere to buy the octopus. After all, it's not the kind of thing you can just whistle up at your neighborhood superstore. If you live in a city with a Chinatown, that's a good place to start. Otherwise, ask your nearest fish store to order one for you.

There are two ways to tenderize fresh octopus before cooking. You can either freeze and thaw it, or you can beat the shit out of it. Actually, make that three ways: the easiest option is to ask the guy who sold it to you to tenderize it for you. Otherwise, spend half an hour going Rocky on that octo, or perhaps flinging it against your garage door, in order to get the flesh nice and supple. You can also put it in the freezer and then let it defrost for a day in the fridge before use. Your call. It depends on how much repressed rage you've got on your hands.

SERVES 6

1 (2-pound) octopus

2 pounds red-skinned potatoes, such as peewees (about 6 medium potatoes)

Kosher salt

1 whole garlic clove, peeled

1 bay leaf

½ tablespoon black peppercorns

½ cup olive oil

5 tablespoons white wine vinegar

2 garlic cloves, crushed

Freshly ground black pepper

Leaves from 1 bunch flat-leaf parsley, chopped

1. Behead the octopus. Slit the head in half and turn it inside out to empty its contents and remove any loosely attached bits (such as the eyes). Remove the beak from the center, where all of the tentacles meet. Rinse the octopus head and tentacles under cold running water.

2. Place the potatoes (whole and unpeeled) in a pressure cooker and add enough water to cover them halfway. Add a pinch of salt. Close and lock the lid of the pressure cooker and place it over high heat. When the pan reaches pressure, reduce the heat to low and set a timer for 15 minutes. When the time is up, release all of the vapor from the pressure cooker and remove the potatoes with tongs, reserving the cooking water. Peel the potatoes while they are as hot as you can handle (the skin should slip off easily).

3. Add enough water to almost totally cover your octopus (just eyeball it), plus the whole garlic clove, bay leaf, and peppercorns and bring the water to a boil. Add the cleaned octopus head and tentacles. Close and lock the lid of the pressure cooker and turn the heat to high until it gets to pressure. Reduce the heat to low and set a timer for 15 minutes. When the time is up, release all of the vapor and check the octopus for tenderness; a fork should sink easily into the thickest part of the flesh. If not, close the top and bring it to pressure for another minute or two and check it again.

4. When the octopus is ready, remove it from the pressure cooker and drain off the liquid. Remove any remaining skin from the octopus by lightly dragging a knife blade on the back end and sides of the tentacles; only remove the skin from the suction-cup side if you want to remove the suction cups, which are a nice decorative flourish if you ask me. Chop up the head and tentacles into small, bite-sized chunks.

5. Prepare a vinaigrette by combining the oil, vinegar, crushed garlic cloves, and salt and pepper to taste in a small jar. Close the lid and shake it to blend.

6. Chop the potatoes into bite-sized chunks and combine them in a bowl along with the octopus, chopped parsley, and vinaigrette. Mix well and serve at room temperature.

6

MEATS

EVERYTHING BUT THE QUACK

DUCK IS ONE OF MY FAVORITE MEATS. Lighter than beef and pork and more flavorful than chicken, these little birds are fantastically tasty, forgiving to cook, and easier than ever to get your hands on in the United States. Still, though, I've seen little in the way of good duck recipes geared toward the home cook. So this chapter offers a few of my favorite uses for every part of the duck—including the eggs, which are big, rich, and gorgeous, like chicken eggs on steroids.

DUCK PROSCIUTTO

We've touched on some charcuterie recipes already—all cooked or pressed stuff—but this is your big chance to cure your own meat. Duck breast is the easiest whole muscle to cure and dry, as it's small enough to do the whole process in a standard fridge. The texture and flavor are wonderfully distinct, and you can use duck prosciutto in loads of different ways, from charcuterie platters to sandwiches and salads. The process takes some patience, but it's cool as fuck knowing you can pull something like this off in your own kitchen.

You might have your doubts about whether you can really hang on to raw meat for upward of a month without it rotting. Well, the duck breasts won't rot, thanks to the salt-curing process. As you watch the breasts dry, keep in mind that white mold is good mold! If you see green mold, wash the afflicted breast in saltwater solution and re-hang it. But you won't get green mold unless it's living somewhere in your fridge already, which is another problem entirely.

MAKES 4 DUCK PROSCIUTTOS

4 (10- to 12-ounce) Pekin or Muscovy duck breasts

2½ teaspoons black peppercorns

2½ teaspoons coriander seeds

1 teaspoon fennel seeds

Pinch of juniper berries

2 pinches of Szechuan peppercorns, optional

1½ cups kosher salt

1 teaspoon pink salt (also called Prague powder #2, or DQ curing salt #2)

¾ cup plus 2 tablespoons sugar

1. Weigh each duck breast and record the weights someplace where you won't lose it.

2. In a small saucepan set over medium heat, toast the black peppercorns, coriander seeds, fennel seeds, juniper berries, and Szechuan peppercorns, if using, until fragrant, 1 to 2 minutes.

3. Coarsely crack the toasted spices using a mortar and pestle or a coffee grinder. Chuck them into a small bowl and mix them thoroughly with the salts and sugar. Pack the duck breasts on all sides with this dry cure, then bury them in the remaining cure inside a sealed plastic container or zip-top bag.

4. Cure the breasts for 24 hours, then remove them from the curing mixture and brush off as much as possible with a kitchen towel. Let the breasts dry uncovered in the refrigerator for 8 hours.

5. Take a length of butcher's twine and tie one end around each breast, or poke a hole in one end of each breast, thread the twine through, and tie a loop. Hang the breasts from a rack in the refrigerator until each breast has lost at least 20 to 25 percent of its weight, 4 to 6 weeks. Thinly slice and serve. It will keep stored in the refrigerator for up to 6 months.

DUCK AND WALNUT TERRINE

I know what you're thinking: "Yeah, right! Good one, knobhead, as if I'm going to bother making this." But this terrine is proper worth it. And it gets better with a bit of age, as all the flavors meld. It's good to eat as soon as it's chilled, two weeks on it's great, and after three it's fantastic. At the one-month mark, though, you should probably get rid of it.

MAKES ONE 8 × 4-INCH TERRINE

4 ounces duck leg meat, diced

2 ounces pork shoulder meat (aka pork butt), diced

1½ ounces pork fatback

1 ounce chicken livers

½ teaspoon kosher salt

¼ teaspoon freshly ground black pepper

¼ teaspoon sugar

½ garlic clove, finely chopped

½ shallot, diced

½ teaspoon fresh thyme leaves

2 tablespoons brandy

2 tablespoons port

2 slices white bread

½ cup heavy cream

⅓ cup walnut pieces

¼ teaspoon pink curing salt (also called Prague powder #2, or DQ curing salt #2)

¾ ounce foie gras, diced

1½ ounces duck breast, diced

1. In a large bowl, combine the duck leg meat, pork shoulder, fatback, chicken livers, kosher salt, black pepper, sugar, garlic, shallot, thyme, brandy, and port. Toss well and cover. Refrigerate for 24 hours. Remove the meat mixture from the fridge, drain it through a fine-mesh sieve, and discard the liquid.

2. Preheat the oven to 325°F.

3. Using a stand mixer with a meat grinder attachment fitted with a ½-inch die, grind the meat once through into a large bowl. In a blender, combine the white bread and cream and blend until smooth. Add the bread mixture to the ground meat, followed by the walnuts, curing salt, foie gras, and duck breast. Mix it up well with your hands.

4. Line the bottom and sides of a large earthenware terrine or 8 × 4-inch loaf pan with plastic wrap, leaving enough of an overhang on all sides of the pan so that the plastic wrap will completely cover the top of the pâté mixture when folded over. Transfer the meat mixture to the terrine mold, pressing it down with your fingers to make sure it's tightly packed. Fold the overlapping plastic wrap over the mixture to encase it. Use a piece of cardboard or a bit of wood to press down so the meat is packed nice and even and you've got out all the excess air.

5. Set the terrine mold in a roasting pan and add boiling water to reach three quarters of the way up the sides. Bake for 1½ hours, or until the internal temperature reaches 165°F. Remove the terrine from the oven, wrap it in aluminum foil, then place a 2- to 3-pound weight on top of it; this is called pressing, and it's very important for packing the pâté nice and tight, removing any air that would cause the pâté to discolor and go bad during the maturing process.

6. Refrigerate the terrine for at least 8 hours. Cut it into ½-inch slices and serve.

ROASTED DUCK BREAST WITH FIGS AND FARRO

Duck is always a big seller on restaurant menus, but for some reason, it doesn't occur to people to cook it for themselves at home. This is a shame, because how much beef, turkey, chicken, and pork can you choke down before getting sick to death of it? Sure, duck is more expensive than chicken, but it's also cheaper than a good-quality steak. And the truth is that duck breast is easier to cook than almost anything, thanks to the ample layer of fat that keeps the meat naturally moist and tender while it roasts.

This is a dish with a restaurant-quality feel but an ease and simplicity to the execution that makes it perfect for banging out at home. It's a great choice when company's coming. Farro, for those unfamiliar, is a type of whole grain wheat that can be prepared like a risotto. Fresh figs are in season from May to October; if you can't get them, substitute an equal volume of apricots, peaches, apples, or pears.

SERVES 4

4 (10- to 12-ounce) duck breasts, ideally Pekin or Muscovy

¼ cup dry sherry

¼ cup sherry vinegar

½ cup chicken stock

2 teaspoons honey

1 teaspoon chopped fresh thyme

Kosher salt and freshly ground black pepper

8 fresh figs, stemmed and cut in half

1 tablespoon unsalted butter

Farrotto (recipe follows)

1. Preheat the oven to 425°F.

2. If your duck breasts still have sinew on them and the fat side hasn't been scored, your butcher is a wanker and you're going to have to do it yourself. With the skin side of the breast facing up, use a very sharp knife to cut through the skin and fat almost to the flesh, forming a grid pattern with the lines ⅛-inch apart. Flip the breast over; if you see any silvery white skin, trim it off as carefully as you can, trying not to remove any meat.

3. Heat a large cast-iron pan over medium-high heat for 1 minute, letting it get good and hot. Place the duck breasts in the pan skin-side down and let the fat begin to render—aka liquefy. After about 6 minutes, when the skin is golden brown, begin basting the tops of the breasts, spooning the rendered fat over them. Continue basting and cooking until much of the fat is rendered and the skin is crisp and deep golden brown, another 2 to 4 minutes.

4. Put the pan in the oven and roast the breasts until cooked through, 3 to 4 minutes. If you want to prod one with a thermometer, it should read 135°F in the center for medium-rare, which is how I recommend serving duck. Transfer the duck breasts to a plate or platter and cover them with foil to rest and keep warm.

5. Pour off the remaining fat and set the pan back on a medium-high burner. Add the sherry and sherry vinegar; scrape the pan with a wooden spoon to release the browned bits, then boil the liquid until reduced to 2 tablespoons, about 3 minutes. Add the stock, honey, and thyme and season with salt and pepper. Boil until the liquid is reduced by about half, about 3 more minutes. Reduce the heat to low and add the figs. Add the butter to the sauce in bits, consistently stirring or swirling the pan.

6. Slice the duck opposite the grain of the muscle fibers into ¾-inch slices and arrange them on a bed of farrotto. Drizzle with the fig pan sauce and serve.

(continued)

FARROTTO

Wild arugula has smaller, spindlier, and more peppery leaves than farmed arugula. It can typically be found at farmers' markets.

SERVES 4

¾ cup farro

6 cups chicken stock

3 tablespoons olive oil

2 tablespoons unsalted butter

1 large or 2 small shallots, chopped

Kosher salt and freshly
ground black pepper

⅓ cup white wine

⅓ cup diced fresh figs

¼ cup pine nuts, toasted

3 handfuls of wild arugula (farmed
arugula can be substituted)

½ cup grated Parmesan

¼ lemon

1. In a medium bowl, soak the farro in 4 cups water for 30 minutes. Drain. Meanwhile, heat the stock in a small saucepan and keep it warm over low heat.

2. In a large saucepan, heat the oil and butter over medium heat until the butter begins to foam. Add the shallots and season with a pinch of salt and a grind of pepper. Cook until softened, about 2 minutes.

3. Add the drained farro and stir constantly until toasted, 3 to 4 minutes. Chuck in the wine and stir constantly until evaporated, about 2 minutes.

4. Begin adding the hot stock a ladleful at a time, stirring the farro constantly until the stock is completely absorbed. Keep adding stock, waiting until one addition is fully absorbed before adding more, until the farro is creamy and cooked through, about 30 minutes. Turn off the heat and stir in the figs, pine nuts, arugula, and Parmesan. Season with salt, pepper, and a squeeze of lemon juice.

DUCK AU VIN

Duck legs are truly delicious; they're basically poultry that thinks it's red meat. The way that people most commonly cook them is confit style, which means simmering them in duck fat. I've found that braising duck legs in beef stock and red wine gives them an even richer, meatier flavor, while making an incredible sauce to serve them with at the same time. If duck isn't your thing, you can use this same exact braise recipe for short ribs, pork shoulder, pig's head, veal breast, or chicken legs (switch the beef broth for chicken broth in that case).

SERVES 4

4 large whole duck legs, trimmed of excess fat

½ teaspoon salt

Freshly ground black pepper

1 teaspoon Chinese five-spice powder

1 tablespoon olive oil

6 garlic cloves, chopped

3 shallots, chopped

1 large onion, chopped

6 sprigs thyme

6 sprigs rosemary

2 bay leaves

2 cups red wine

8 cups low-sodium beef broth

1½ cups orange juice

1. Pat the duck legs dry with paper towels and sprinkle them with the salt, pepper to taste, and the five-spice powder.

2. In a Dutch oven large enough to fit the duck legs in a single layer, heat the oil over medium-high heat until it shimmers. Add the duck legs skin-side down and cook without touching them until the skin is deep golden brown and crisp, about 15 minutes. Turn the legs over and cook them for an additional 2 minutes, then transfer them to a plate.

3. Preheat the oven to 325°F.

4. Add the garlic, shallots, and onion to the Dutch oven and cook over medium heat until softened, about 5 minutes. Add the thyme, rosemary, and bay leaves and cook, stirring, for 3 minutes more. Pour off all but 2 tablespoons of the fat.

5. Add the wine and bring to a boil, scraping up the lovely browned bits that will have stuck to the bottom of the pan. Continue to boil the mixture until reduced by half, about 10 minutes. Return the duck legs to the pan, skin side up, and add the broth and orange juice. Bring the liquid to a simmer, cover the pot, and transfer it to the oven. After 20 minutes, lower the temperature to 300°F. Cook for 45 minutes, then check the liquid level; if it's beginning to dry out, top it off with beef stock until the duck legs are more than halfway submerged. Braise until very tender, about 1 hour more.

6. Transfer the duck legs to a plate, and if there's lots of excess fat on the surface of the cooking liquid, remove some with a spoon. Strain the liquid through a fine-mesh sieve, rinse out the Dutch oven, and return the cooking liquid back to the pot, pressing hard on the solids to extract all the delicious liquid. Boil the pan sauce until it's reduced by one third and slightly thickened, about 10 minutes. Serve the duck legs drizzled with pan sauce.

GRILLED ASPARAGUS WITH FRIED DUCK EGGS

I don't cook at home as much as you might think, just like I'm sure a carpenter doesn't rush home from work to build himself a new shed. I did, however, go and buy a spiffy grill for the garden that features a double burner on the side, on the premise that if I'm going to be cooking on my own time, I might as well be outdoors as much as possible while I'm doing it. For a recipe like this one, which includes a mix of stovetop and grill cooking, a grill like mine saves a lot of running about.

Duck eggs are colossal compared with the hen eggs we're all used to, with gorgeous, fatty, rich yolks. Do make a reasonable effort to find them (in better grocery stores, for instance), as they're pretty spectacular. They're key to setting this dish apart, as is the duck prosciutto—which I'm sure you all started on six weeks ago, right? Of course, if need be, hen eggs and store-bought prosciutto or country ham can be substituted and the whole thing will still be delicious.

SERVES 4

2 large bunches jumbo green asparagus (16 spears total)

1 tablespoon olive oil, plus more for drizzling

1 garlic clove, minced

Sea salt

2 tablespoons unsalted butter

8 fresh duck eggs (chicken eggs may be substituted)

4 ounces freshly grated Parmesan

16 to 20 paper-thin slices Duck Prosciutto (page 96; regular prosciutto may be substituted)

Freshly ground black pepper

¼ lemon

1. Light your grill for medium-high-heat cooking. Snap off and discard the woody bases from the asparagus. In a large bowl, toss the asparagus with the oil, garlic, and salt to taste. Make sure that you rub the oil onto the asparagus evenly.

2. Cook the asparagus on the grill with the lid down for 5 minutes, turning it just once; we want some char marks from the grill bars to help cut the richness of the eggs and cheese.

3. Heat a large cast-iron or nonstick pan over medium-high heat, add the butter, and wait until it begins to foam. Add the eggs to the hot butter 4 at a time and sprinkle them with salt and pepper. Cook them until the whites are opaque but the yolks are still runny. Transfer the eggs to a paper towel and cook the second batch.

4. Remove the asparagus from the grill and either divide it among 4 plates or platter the whole lot. Sprinkle the asparagus with Parmesan and lay the fried eggs on top. Sprinkle more Parmesan, followed by the duck prosciutto and a last layer of Parmesan. Drizzle the dish with oil, add a dash of salt, a grind of pepper, and a squeeze of lemon juice.

THE PIG

PORK WAS THE MOST POPULAR MEAT IN THE UNITED STATES UNTIL WORLD WAR II, when it was eclipsed by beef, and that by chicken in 2014. If you care to thumb through the index of this book, you can see where my loyalties lie. One chicken recipe; three for beef; for pork, nine.

Such is my love for all parts of the pig that I could write a whole book on pork, but I've somehow managed to restrain myself and start you lads off with just a few really solid recipes, the crème de la crème of my pig dossier—including a mind-blowingly tender slow-cooked pork shoulder and a salty-sweet rack of grilled pork ribs that will leave you saying "Cow, who?"

PRESSURE COOKER CASSOULET

At my restaurants, we always cook our dried beans in a pressure cooker because it makes them super tender, and they don't burst through their skins the way they sometimes can when you boil them in water. That got me thinking about making cassoulet—that hearty winter stew of beans and pork from the southwest of France—in the same fashion. This recipe gets you all the same gloriously rich flavors of a slow-cooked cassoulet, only it won't take you all day.

SERVES 4

3 tablespoons blended vegetable oil

1½ pounds pork butt, cut into 1-inch cubes

Kosher salt and freshly ground black pepper

2 (4-ounce) pork sausages (any kind will do, but preferably raw)

10 tablespoons unsalted butter

1 large yellow onion, diced

3 garlic cloves

2 sprigs thyme

1 sprig rosemary

2 bay leaves

1 tablespoon fennel seeds

1 tablespoon tomato paste

5 vine ripe tomatoes, peeled and chopped

1½ cups white wine

4 drops of Tabasco sauce

5 tablespoons Worcestershire sauce

1 cup white beans (such as cannellini, tarbais, Great Northern, runner, or gigante), soaked overnight in cold water to cover by a couple inches

4 cups chicken stock

2 tablespoons *fines herbes* (equal parts tarragon, chervil, and chives), coarsely chopped

1. Heat the oil in a pressure cooker set over high heat. Season the pork butt well and sear it until browned on all sides, 5 to 7 minutes. Transfer the meat to a plate and sear the sausages on all sides, about 5 minutes. Transfer them as well.

2. Reduce the heat to medium and add half of the butter. When it starts to foam, add the onions, garlic, thyme, rosemary, bay leaves, and fennel seeds. Sweat the herbs and veggies until soft and fragrant. Add the tomato paste and cook, stirring, for 1 minute.

3. Stir in the chopped tomatoes followed by the wine, using a wooden spoon or spatula to scrape the browned bits from the bottom of the pan. Let the wine simmer and reduce until almost dry, 10 to 15 minutes.

4. Add the Tabasco sauce, Worcestershire sauce, and remaining butter. Return the pork and sausages to the cooker. Add the beans and chicken stock. Bring it to a boil and close the lid on the pressure cooker according to the manufacturer's instructions.

5. Place the cooker under high pressure according to the manufacturer's instructions and cook for 45 minutes. Depressurize the cooker, remove the lid, and stir through the *fines herbs*. Serve immediately.

CHARCUTERIE:
HOW TO ASSEMBLE THE ULTIMATE MEAT BOARD

I've loved charcuterie from the moment I could chew. The English excel at all manner of potted meats, sausages, terrines, and bacon, of course, and I was blessed to have an Italian aunt who would go to Italy every summer and return to England with mortadella, prosciutto, and salami in tow, all of which I devoured with abandon.

I've worked at mastering the dark art of charcuterie ever since I started cooking as a teenager, and twenty-plus years later, I'm still learning. Curing meat is an intense, technical, and time-consuming process, hard for even restaurants to get right. With all the phenomenal craft charcuterie outfits out there today, I can't say that I recommend making your own at home. But one of the more underappreciated facets of being a good cook is becoming a discerning shopper. There is an art to putting together the ultimate selection of meats, which I'll endeavor to pass on to you here.

The term *charcuterie* encompasses all preserved meats, most of which came about as peasant dishes aimed at using up the uglier bits of animals, turning scraps and odd cuts into something very delicious as well as long-lasting. These days, of course, terrines, pâtés, cured meats, and the like are treated as luxury foods. A good charcuterie spread is a beautiful thing to behold, a pure and simple pleasure delivery system.

First, let's survey the meatscape. Charcuterie goes beyond prosciutto, lads! I divide it into the following categories:

- Dried salamis, such as Spanish chorizo, Italian soppressata, and French saucisson sec

- Whole muscles, such as prosciutto, speck, coppa, bresaola, bacon, and jamón ibérico

- Pâtés, terrines, and mousses

- Smoked sausages, such as bratwurst or kielbasa

- Cold cooked sausages, such as mortadella

- Confit meat, such as potted meats or rillettes

Putting together a killer spread is all about balance. Try for a diversity of textures and flavors, working across the above categories as widely as possible. You'll want something spicy, something salty, and something really fatty and unctuous. Try to represent a range of species too: pork, beef, duck, even rabbit and goose. Then you've got something for everyone, and you'll almost certainly introduce your mates to a delicious cut or preparation they've never tried before.

You may decide to really throw some weight behind the meat plate effort and make a terrine or mousse yourself, but for cured meats, you're best off leaving it to any one of a number of craft charcuterie operations that have popped up all over the country. Molinari, Boccalone, Olympic Provisions, Olli, and Benton's are among my favorite producers, but they're just the tip of the iceberg. There are new and excellent brands popping up all the time.

If you're buying your meats over a counter, always ask to try a sample before you buy, since so much of what you select simply comes down to personal taste. A good rule of thumb, no matter what your preferences: if it's cheap, don't buy it.

How many types of meat you include depends upon how many people you're feeding. For a small group, a couple of salamis of different diameters, one or two pâtés, and one or two whole muscles (like prosciutto, speck, or bresaola) will do it, but the sky is the limit. At one point, at my restaurant Waterloo & City, we were serving a plate called "The King" with twenty-five different types of house-made charcuterie on it. We had two guys working on our meats full-time, and they were curing and preserving anything that moved.

After you select your meats, then it's all about adding plenty of acid to balance all the fat and salt. Piccalilli, Branston pickle, savory jams, Pickled Mustard Seeds (page 20), caper berries, cornichons, Tomato Confit (page 31), and Preserved Lemons (page 23) are all at home on a charcuterie board. And finally, I always offer both crispy crackers and crusty sliced bread along with the meats.

Now, doesn't that feel like a hell of a lot of work, even if you haven't cooked a thing? Told you so.

THAI-SPICED PORK BELLY WITH FISH SAUCE CARAMEL

I'll admit that this dish is ridiculously labor-intensive for home cooking purposes, but it's so bloody delicious that I felt compelled to write the whole thing out for you anyway. It's a sort of homage to an incredible catfish dish that I ate at The Slanted Door, Charles Phan's Vietnamese restaurant in San Francisco. This is a pork belly version of that dish.

We cook the pork belly using a technique that is a kind of poor man's sous vide. The idea is to wrap the belly in layer upon layer of plastic wrap, followed by several layers of aluminum foil, and then roast it partially submerged in water. It's a cross between sous vide—the cooking method that involves vacuum sealing an ingredient and cooking it for very long periods submerged in warm water—and braising, where you roast something partly submerged in stock or wine. Braising dilutes the flavor of meat by letting its juices run out and be replaced by the wine or stock you're cooking it in; I find that meat cooked sous vide has a flat, gummy texture to it. This method improves on both, allowing the meat to almost confit in its own rendered fat and juices, keeping it tender and moist and maintaining a powerful flavor of pork.

At the very end, the pork belly bits get dunked in the fryer so they'll be crispy on the outside and pudding-soft on the inside, then lacquered with a salty-sweet fish sauce caramel.

SERVES 12 AS A NIBBLE

1 (3- to 5-pound) skinless pork belly

1 cup Thai-Spiced Pork Belly Rub (recipe follows)

Cooking oil

1 cup Fish Sauce Caramel (recipe follows)

1. Massage the pork belly thoroughly with the rub. Let it sit covered in the refrigerator for at least 24 and no more than 48 hours.

2. Give the pork a good wash and soak it under cold running water for 20 to 25 minutes. Pat it dry.

3. Pull a piece of plastic wrap out onto a clean work surface and roll the pork belly in plastic no fewer than two or three times, keeping the belly as flat as possible. Turn the belly 180 degrees and wrap it in two or three more layers of plastic. Now repeat the process using aluminum foil. You'll end up with what looks like an enormous brick of cocaine.

4. Preheat the oven to 275°F.

5. Place the pork belly package in a large roasting pan and pour hot water in to reach halfway up the belly. Place the roasting pan on the stovetop and bring the water to a boil over high heat. Carefully transfer the pan to the oven and cook it for 4 hours, topping off the water as necessary to keep it at around the same level. Remove it from oven and allow it to rest for 1 hour.

6. Transfer the pork belly from the roasting pan to a high-sided baking sheet. Poke a few holes in the plastic and foil and drain off the juices (save and refrigerate them for later—beautiful on toast!). Unwrap the meat once it's cool enough to handle.

7. If you've got an electric fryer by chance, use it, because they're way safer; if not, use a heavy pot like a Dutch oven. Fill the fryer or pot half full with cooking oil. Position a thermometer in the oil and heat it nice and slow over medium heat until the temperature reads 350°F.

8. Cut the pork belly into 2-inch squares. Working a few pieces at a time, fry them until golden and crisp, 3 to 4 minutes. Remove them from the fryer to a paper towel. Glaze with the fish sauce caramel either by brushing it on all sides or using a slotted spoon to submerge the pork belly in a bowl of the caramel. Eat immediately.

THAI-SPICED PORK BELLY RUB

MAKES 1 CUP

8 cloves

Good pinch of fennel seeds

½ teaspoon coriander seeds

1 garlic clove

1 stalk lemongrass, peeled of its tough outer layers and sliced

½ cup kosher salt

1 teaspoon pink curing salt (also called Prague powder #2, or DQ curing salt #2)

¼ cup sugar

Pinch of smoked Spanish paprika

1 teaspoon Chinese five-spice powder

Zest of 1 lemon, lime, and orange

1. In a small skillet over medium-low heat, toast the cloves, fennel seeds, and coriander seeds for a minute or two, until they begin to pop and turn fragrant. Grind them coarsely using a mortar and pestle or a spice grinder.

2. Add the garlic and lemongrass and break them down to a paste.

3. Add the salts, sugar, paprika, five-spice powder, and citrus zests and mix well.

FISH SAUCE CARAMEL

MAKES 1 CUP

1 tablespoon canola oil

¼ stalk lemongrass, peeled of tough outer layers and thinly sliced

1 small garlic clove, finely chopped

½ shallot, finely diced

1 large Fresno chile, seeded and finely diced

½ tablespoon peeled finely diced ginger

1 teaspoon coriander seeds

1 cup granulated sugar

¼ cup Thai fish sauce

1 tablespoon rice wine vinegar

½ tablespoon fresh lemon juice

1 tablespoon chopped fresh cilantro

1. Heat the canola oil in a medium heavy-bottomed saucepot set over medium heat. Add the lemongrass, garlic, shallot, chile, ginger, and coriander seeds and cook for 5 to 10 minutes, until soft.

2. Add the sugar to pan and let it melt and turn a medium amber color, 5 to 10 minutes. Watch it closely, as it will go from clear to burned in the blink of an eye.

3. As soon as the sugar is medium amber in color, dump in the fish sauce and vinegar and bring to a boil—careful, it will spit and sputter. Stir to dissolve any lumps of caramel.

4. Allow the caramel to cool to room temperature, then add the lemon juice and cilantro. Use it warm; it will keep in the fridge for at least a month.

SLOW-COOKED PORK SHOULDER

There's little that compares to the carnivorous pleasure of sinking your teeth into meltingly tender, salty, sweet, spicy slow-cooked pork. This is a recipe that we developed for a happy hour sandwich at Waterloo & City, and we literally couldn't cook enough of it to keep up with demand.

The paradox of big, heavily used muscles like leg and shoulder roasts of beef, lamb, or pork is that the longer you cook them at low temperatures, the more tender they become. That's because they contains a lot of collagen, which melts in the heat and bastes and tenderizes the muscle fibers while they cook; after 8 or 10 hours, you can pull apart a pork shoulder with only so much as a fork. These cuts are supremely low-maintenance, as you can pop them in the oven and forget about them without worrying that you'll overcook dinner. Keep in mind that cooking low and slow only works with collagen-rich meats—so don't try to do it with your Thanksgiving turkey, which will turn into a proper nightmare of scorched, tough flesh if left in the oven for a couple extra hours.

SERVES 8 TO 10

¼ cup kosher salt

1½ tablespoons brown sugar

3½ tablespoons smoked Spanish paprika

1 tablespoon mustard powder

1 tablespoon onion powder

1 tablespoon garlic powder

1½ teaspoons chili powder

1½ teaspoons ground cumin

1 (6- to 8-pound) boneless pork shoulder (if using bone-in, add another hour to the cooking time)

Chuck the salt, brown sugar, and spices into a small bowl and toss them together until evenly combined. Lay the pork shoulder on a clean work surface and pack it all over with the spice mixture, making sure to hit all the nooks and crevices. Transfer it to a zip-top bag or a sealed storage container and refrigerate it for no less than 8 hours, no more than 24 hours.

TO COOK IT IN THE OVEN:

1. Remove the shoulder from the refrigerator and allow it to come to room temperature, about 1 hour; preheat the oven to 250°F during the last 20 minutes.

2. Place the shoulder in a roasting pan fatty-side up and pour about ½ inch of water into the pan. Roast until the meat's internal temperature reaches 165°F, 6 to 8 hours (for super-tender pulled pork, push it an hour or two further to 195°F). Add more water to the pan if it dries out during cooking. Remove the shoulder from the oven, cover with foil, and let it rest for 30 minutes to catch the steam as it cools.

3. Slice the roast or pull the meat apart with a fork and serve.

TO COOK IT ON THE GRILL:

1. If you have a gas grill, light one side and preheat the grill to a temperature between 210 and 250°F (the lower the better). For a charcoal grill, light a pile of coals on one half of the grill and wait for the temperature to fall below 250°F. Meanwhile, remove the shoulder from the refrigerator and allow to come to room temperature, about 1 hour.

2. Place the shoulder fat-side up on the cool side of the grill and position an aluminum pan filled with a couple of inches of water on the rack above it; this will allow the shoulder to baste itself as it cooks. Doing your best to keep the grill temperature between 210 and 250°F, cook the roast to an internal temperature of at least 165°F.

This can take anywhere from 6 to 12 hours, depending on the weight of the roast and the grill temperature; expect 90 minutes per pound at 225°F. Add more water to the aluminum pan if it runs dry. Remove the shoulder from the grill, cover with foil to catch the steam as it cools, and let it rest for 30 minutes.

3. Slice the roast or pull the meat apart with a fork and serve.

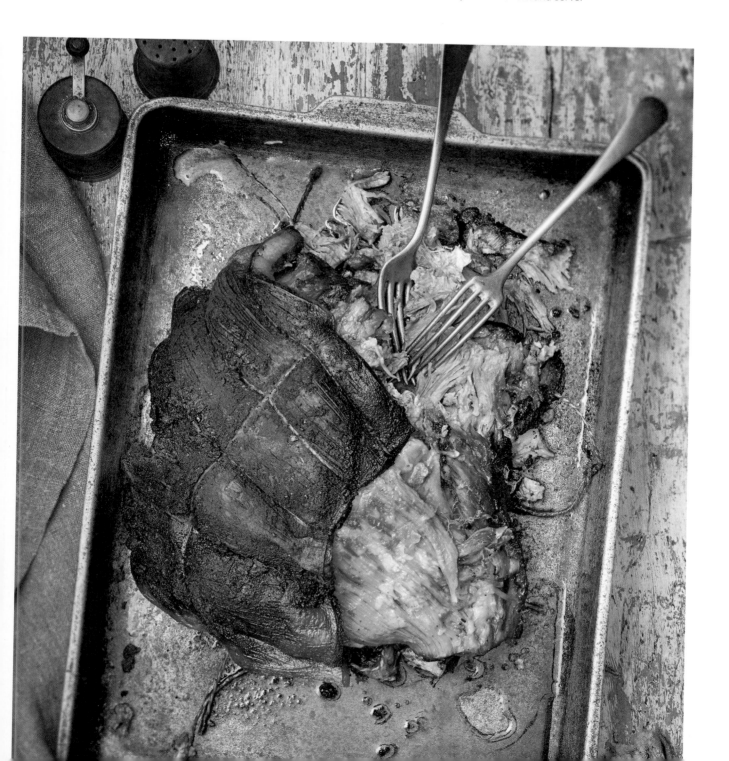

DEAD-EASY PORK RIBS WITH PALM SUGAR GLAZE

Chinese five-spice powder is one of my all-time favorite seasonings, and I encourage you to get very friendly with it. It takes its name not from the number of ingredients, but the way this single spice mix hits on all five principal tastes (sweet, salty, sour, bitter, and umami). The flavor is warm and sweet, and I find that it acts like a bridge between salt and the heat of chiles, giving these ribs a really round, warm deliciousness. It's a wonderful, versatile seasoning to add to pork, beef, or duck. Chinese five-spice powder also lends meat a handsome reddish tone—like that nice red bark that you get when you put meat in a smoker—which is a big improvement over the unappetizing gray tinge that ribs can take on when they're cooked in the oven.

SERVES 6

2 racks St. Louis-style pork ribs

Kosher salt and freshly ground black pepper

2 teaspoons Chinese five-spice powder

1 cup Palm Sugar Caramel (recipe follows)

1. Preheat the oven to 225°F.

2. Season your ribs on both sides very simply with salt and pepper and dust with the Chinese five-spice powder.

3. Place the ribs meat-side down in a pair of aluminum or glass baking dishes. Cover the dishes with aluminum foil and roast the meat for 4 hours.

4. Drain off the drippings. Flip the ribs over using two spatulas (and an extra pair of hands, if you have them) so the meat side is now up. Be gentle, as they may be so tender they start falling apart. Paint a layer of palm sugar caramel on the ribs and return them to the oven uncovered for an additional 20 to 30 minutes. Serve straight out of the oven.

PALM SUGAR CARAMEL
MAKES ABOUT 1½ CUPS

2 cups palm sugar

1 tablespoon fresh lemon juice

2 cups thinly sliced shallots (from 4 to 6 large shallots)

1 dried hot red chile, such as chile de árbol

3 star anise

1 cinnamon stick

2 teaspoons freshly ground black pepper

½ cup Thai fish sauce

1. In a heavy-bottomed medium saucepan set over medium heat, combine the palm sugar, lemon juice, and ¼ cup water and bring the mixture to a boil. Using a wet pastry brush, wash down any sugar crystals that have stuck to the side of the pan. Reduce the heat to medium-low and let the mixture simmer undisturbed until it begins to reach a medium amber color, about 20 minutes (watch the pot carefully, because caramel can go from pale to burned in a matter of seconds).

2. Remove the saucepan from the heat and stir in the shallots, chile, star anise, cinnamon, and black pepper. Carefully whisk in the fish sauce and another ¼ cup water—the caramel will seize up and spit. Return the pan to medium heat and stir it until the caramel is smooth and dissolved. Pour it into a heatproof bowl and let it cool completely. Remove the chile, star anise, and cinnamon stick and use while warm.

ROASTED PIG'S HEAD

Admittedly, a severed head doesn't scream "delicious" (technically it doesn't scream anything—ha, ha!). The first time I saw my granddad roast a pig's head, I honestly assumed that it was for the dog, and I felt sorry for the poor bastard. But once I got a taste of the crispy skin, melt-in-your-mouth jowls, tongue, cheeks, and even a bit of creamy brain served with mashed potatoes and applesauce, I have to admit that I became a twelve-year-old believer. So man up and have a go! Brining really helps to take away the livery tang that you get with cuts like these, so I'm doing you a solid here that granddad never did for me.

SERVES 2 TO 3

---

1 whole pig's head, split (Either have your butcher do the honors, or do it at home with a wood saw. I've tried a chainsaw and it's too messy, lads.)

1 gallon Pork Brine (recipe follows)

1 small carrot, finely chopped

½ onion, finely chopped

1 leek, white part only, finely chopped

3 ribs celery, finely chopped

1. First things first: pig heads come hairy, so you've either got to give this puppy a shave or blowtorch the hair off him. Burning hair stinks to high heaven, so I recommend going the Gillette route. No shaving cream necessary.

2. Brining time! In 2 zip-top bags or large containers of some description, submerge each half of the head in the pork brine. Refrigerate them for at least 24 hours and no more than 5 days.

3. Time for a wash! Put the head in the sink inside a bowl of clean cold water and let the faucet run on top to keep circulating fresh cold water. The longer the brine, the longer the wash—15 minutes per 24 hours is a good guideline.

4. Preheat the oven to 300°F.

5. Pull a piece of plastic wrap out onto a clean work surface and roll one of the head halves in plastic no fewer than 2 or 3 times. Turn it 180 degrees and wrap it in 2 or 3 more layers of plastic. Now do the same thing with aluminum foil. Repeat the process for the other half.

6. Place both head halves flat-side down in a large roasting pan and pour hot water in to reach halfway up them. Place the roasting pan on the stovetop and bring the water to a boil over high heat. Carefully transfer the pan to the oven and cook for 4 hours, topping off the water as necessary to keep it at around the same level. Remove the roasting pan from the oven and allow it to rest for 30 minutes.

7. Turn your oven temperature up to 375°F. Spread the chopped vegetables evenly on a fresh roasting pan or baking sheet, unwrap the head halves, and arrange them flat-side down on top of the vegetables. Roast until the skin is golden and crisp, 45 to 60 minutes.

8. Serve the head (and vegetables, if you fancy) with mashed potatoes and applesauce. Everything in the head but the bones is edible, so dig in.

PORK BRINE
MAKES 1 GALLON

1 gallon water

1 cup kosher salt

½ cup brown sugar

¼ cup coriander seeds

3 tablespoons black peppercorns

2 tablespoons cloves

6 bay leaves

8 garlic cloves

1 lemon peel

1 orange peel

4 star anise

1 cinnamon stick

1 bunch cilantro stems

½ cup dried whole chiles,
such as chiles de árbol

Combine all the ingredients in a large stockpot and bring to a boil over high heat. Reduce the heat to medium and let the mixture simmer for 10 minutes, then remove it from the heat, cool completely, and chill it to fridge-cold before use.

VEGGIES

IF THERE'S ONE MALE STEREOTYPE I'M EAGER TO PUT TO REST, it's the one that says we're all Neanderthals interested in cooking and eating only meat. Yes, meat is easy to love, but I know plenty of blokes who appreciate a ripe local tomato with a little sea salt and olive oil or root vegetables roasted golden and sweet. Including me.

Unlike meat, most vegetables on their own don't have much in the way of umami: that rich, savory flavor that makes food taste substantial. Learning to prepare them to maximize their depth of flavor—browning or grilling them, for instance, or complementing them with ingredients like cheese, vinegar, or oil—is key to making them really shine. What follows is a rock-solid selection of vegetable options for every time of year, from evergreen dishes like Caesar salad and roasted cauliflower to a salt-baked corn on the cob that's unbeatable at the height of summer.

ARUGULA SALAD WITH SMOKED ALMONDS AND CRISPY SHALLOTS

Right lads, salad time: this one doesn't feel like diet food thanks to the Parmesan and bits of fried shallot sprinkled throughout (far fresher versions of those atrociously unhealthy but totally addictive French's Fried Onion Rings that your mum might have put on her green bean casserole). If you're pressed for time, you can skip the shallots and you've got a salad that comes together in under fifteen minutes and still has plenty of flavor and texture to spare from the almonds, cheese, and rock-solid balsamic vinaigrette.

SERVES 4 TO 6

4 large shallots, peeled

1 cup whole milk

Canola oil for frying

2 cups all-purpose flour (use Wondra flour or 00 flour for extra-crispy shallots)

Table salt for seasoning

8 ounces wild arugula (about 4 big handfuls)

1½ to 2 cups smoked almonds

1½ cups grated Parmesan

Balsamic Vinaigrette (page 126)

Kosher salt and freshly ground black pepper

1. Shave the shallots very thinly with a Japanese mandoline or sharp knife; separate the rings. Soak the shallots in the milk for at least 30 minutes to remove some of their sharpness.

2. Fill a Dutch oven or other heavy-bottomed pot with 2 to 3 inches of oil. Position a thermometer in the oil and heat it nice and slow over medium heat until the temperature reads 350°F.

3. Drain the shallots well, then toss them in flour (this is called dredging). Bounce them around in a metal sieve for a bit to shake the excess flour off. Place the shallots in the oil, stirring them constantly with a slotted spoon and making sure they don't stick together, until golden brown, about 1 to 2 minutes. Using a slotted spoon, transfer them to a paper towel-lined baking sheet to absorb the excess grease. Season with salt while hot. Allow them to cool and use them immediately, or store them in an airtight container for up to 2 days.

4. Wash the arugula and chuck it in a large bowl. Sprinkle the smoked almonds, fried shallots, and Parmesan over the top. Drizzle your dressing around the edges of the bowl, and in a clockwise motion, turn the salad until all the leaves and garnishes are evenly dressed. Taste your salad and season with salt and pepper as needed—that's right, salad needs a touch of salt just like everything else!

BUTTER LETTUCE SALAD WITH HONEY MUSTARD DRESSING

The thing about salads is that we know we're supposed to be eating them, but the fancy versions you find in so many cookbooks and restaurants these days are bitter and sour and not very pleasant to eat. This is a good, honest salad without all the weird bells and whistles—just sweet, delicious butter lettuce. Let's not kid ourselves: there is very little nutritional value in lettuce of any kind, but it's the perfect vehicle to transport oil, vinegar, and mustard, all of which are good for our stomachs and livers.

SERVES 2

FOR THE SALAD DRESSING:

1 garlic clove, peeled and sliced in half

1 tablespoon Dijon mustard

1 tablespoon honey

3 tablespoons white wine vinegar

Salt and freshly ground black pepper

1 cup extra-virgin olive oil

FOR THE SALAD:

1 head butter lettuce (organic/hydroponic is best, but don't beat yourself up about it)

1 shallot, thinly sliced, optional

½ cup croutons (see Note), optional

Leaves from ½ bunch flat-leaf parsley, optional

4 breakfast radishes, sliced, optional

1. Make the dressing: Get out a small bowl and rub the sides with garlic, then toss out the spent clove. Whisk together the mustard, honey, vinegar, and salt and pepper to taste for a minute (be sure to add the salt at this stage, because it won't dissolve once the oil is added). Add the oil in a slow, constant stream, whisking all the while. Transfer the dressing to a bottle or mason jar.

2. Make the salad: Give your lettuce a quick rinse under cold water, then tear the leaves down into manageable pieces. Toss those in a big bowl along with whatever garnishes you're using: I suggest shallots, croutons, parsley, and radishes, but don't limit yourself. Drizzle your dressing around the edges of the bowl, never directly onto the leaves, as it will puddle up in the lettuce and you'll end up with an uneven distribution of dressing. In a clockwise motion, turn the salad until all the leaves and garnishes are evenly dressed. Season with salt and pepper.

3. Serve immediately; the moment the vinegar hits those leaves they start to go limp, and nobody likes a limp salad.

Note: To make croutons: Preheat the oven to 325°F. Cut the crust off any bread and slice it into 1-inch cubes. Figure on ¼ cup bread cubes per person. Toss the cubes in just enough oil to lightly coat them and spread them in a single layer on a baking sheet. Bake them until golden brown and crisp throughout, anywhere from 5 to 15 minutes depending on the size of your cubes. Use them immediately.

CAESAR SALAD

In my first year of cooking school we were sent out to do a work placement in a local professional kitchen. I was lucky enough to be sent to one of the better restaurants in Nottingham and was subsequently opened up to cuisine that was very different from the meat and potatoes I was used to: things like roast duck, fresh tuna, and Caesar salad. Caesar salad seems a bit old-fashioned these days, but it was avant-garde stuff in the north of England in the early 90s.

The Caesar is aptly named, because it truly is the king of salads; I don't care whether or not it's considered trendy these days. Keep in mind that the salad itself is basically just a delivery mechanism for the dressing, so whatever you do, don't "cheat" with a store-bought version. Dress it with oil and vinegar before you do that.

SERVES 4

1 loaf sourdough bread for croutons

Extra-virgin olive oil

2 hearts of romaine, large outer leaves removed

4 large eggs

1½ cups grated Parmesan

2 tablespoons chopped fresh chives

1 cup Caesar Dressing (recipe follows)

Salt and freshly ground black pepper

4 marinated Spanish white anchovies

1. Preheat the oven to 325°F.

2. Make the croutons: Cut the crust off the bread and slice it into roughly ½-inch cubes. Toss them in just enough oil to lightly coat and spread them in a single layer on a baking sheet. Bake until golden brown and crisp throughout, about 10 minutes depending on the exact size of your cubes. Let them cool.

3. Dice the romaine leaves or slice them into strips, being careful to avoid the core at the bottom of the heart.

4. Heat a splash of oil in a cast-iron or Teflon skillet over medium-high heat and fry each egg until the whites are opaque but the yolks are still runny; season with salt and pepper while they cook. Hold them in a warm place while you dress your salad.

5. In a medium bowl, combine the lettuce, 1 cup of the Parmesan, the croutons, chives, and one quarter of the dressing to start off. Mix well, taste, and add more dressing as desired. Season with salt and pepper.

6. Divide the salad among plates or bowls and top with a fried egg, white anchovy, and more Parmesan.

CAESAR DRESSING

MAKES 2 CUPS

½ garlic clove

1 salted anchovy fillet

2 teaspoons white wine vinegar

1½ teaspoons Worcestershire sauce

1 teaspoon Dijon mustard

Drop of Tabasco sauce

¾ cup grated Parmesan

1 large egg yolk

1 cup blended vegetable oil

4 teaspoons warm water

Salt and freshly ground black pepper

1. Chuck the garlic, anchovy, vinegar, Worcestershire sauce, mustard, and Tabasco into a blender and puree until smooth.

2. Scrape the puree into a food processor and add the Parmesan and egg yolk. Blend for 1 minute. While the machine is running, add the oil in a slow, steady stream. As the dressing begins to thicken, alternate the stream of oil with teaspoons of warm water to keep the dressing from getting too thick and separating. Season with salt and pepper; use immediately or refrigerate for up to 3 days.

SOME VINAIGRETTES

Any salad dressing that you make yourself is going to be better than store-bought ones designed to sit on a shelf for eons, so why overpay for a pretty label on a bottle full of chemicals and stabilizers? Roll up your sleeves and make your own. It needn't be complicated.

There are two basic types of vinaigrettes: emulsified and broken. Emulsified vinaigrettes tend to be three parts oil to one part vinegar and often use mustard or egg yolk to help the oil and vinegar blend and stay together. They are opaque, thick, and creamy, and therefore best for sturdy lettuces like iceberg or romaine that can stand up to a dressing with a lot of body. Broken vinaigrettes are usually equal parts oil and vinegar. While the two elements never fully combine as in an emulsified version, shaking them up just before use intersperses the oil and vinegar in little droplets. Broken vinaigrettes are thin and runny, which makes them perfect for delicate lettuces like Bibb, arugula, or field greens.

The acidity of these vinaigrettes keeps them from going off, so they'll stay good to use in your refrigerator until they're finished.

FRENCH VINAIGRETTE

MAKES 3 CUPS

½ cup Dijon mustard

½ cup white wine vinegar

1¼ teaspoons salt, plus more if needed

8 turns of the pepper mill

2 cups canola or blended vegetable oil

In a medium bowl, combine the mustard, vinegar, salt, and pepper. Whisk the vinegar mixture while slowly drizzling in the oil. Taste and add more salt if needed.

SHERRY VINAIGRETTE

MAKES 2 CUPS

1½ teaspoons Dijon mustard

¼ cup sherry vinegar

2½ tablespoons red wine vinegar

2 tablespoons water

2 tablespoons fresh lemon juice

½ garlic clove, grated on a Microplane

1 shallot, finely diced

1 teaspoon salt, plus more if needed

5 turns of the pepper mill

1¼ cups canola or blended vegetable oil

1. In a medium bowl, combine everything but the oil.

2. Whisk the vinegar mixture while slowly drizzling in the oil. For an emulsified vinaigrette, use a handheld blender instead of a whisk. Either way, shake the dressing well just before use. Taste and add more salt if needed.

(continued)

TRUFFLE VINAIGRETTE

MAKES ABOUT 2½ CUPS

½ garlic clove, grated on a Microplane

¼ shallot, finely diced

½ tablespoon grainy mustard

¼ cup Banyuls vinegar

1 tablespoon red wine vinegar

Juice of ½ lemon

¼ cup truffle juice

1 teaspoon salt, plus more if needed

5 turns of the pepper mill

2 tablespoons black or white truffle oil

2 cups canola or blended vegetable oil

1½ ounces canned truffle peelings, or fresh black truffle, finely chopped

1. In a medium bowl, combine the garlic, shallot, mustard, vinegars, lemon juice, truffle juice, salt, and pepper.

2. Whisk the vinegar mixture while slowly drizzling in the oils. For an emulsified vinaigrette, use a handheld blender instead of a whisk. Once all the oil is incorporated, mix in the truffle peelings. Taste and add more salt if needed.

RED WINE VINAIGRETTE

MAKES ABOUT 2 CUPS

¼ cup red wine

1½ teaspoons Dijon mustard

¼ cup Cabernet Sauvignon vinegar or other good red wine vinegar

2 tablespoons fresh lemon juice

¼ garlic clove, grated on a Microplane

½ shallot, finely diced

1 teaspoon kosher salt, plus more if needed

6 turns of the pepper mill

1¼ cups canola or blended vegetable oil

1. In a small saucepan over medium-high heat, reduce the wine by half, about 5 minutes.

2. In a medium bowl, combine the reduced wine, mustard, vinegar, lemon juice, garlic, shallot, salt, and pepper. Whisk the vinegar mixture while slowly drizzling in the oil. Taste and add more salt if needed.

BALSAMIC VINAIGRETTE

MAKES 2¼ CUPS

½ cup good balsamic vinegar

¼ cup red wine vinegar

Juice of ½ lemon

½ teaspoon Dijon mustard

2½ teaspoons kosher salt

10 turns of the pepper mill

2 ounces seasonal fruit such as plums, figs, or apricots, finely chopped, optional

1½ cups canola or blended vegetable oil

Place all the ingredients except the oil in a medium bowl. Using a whisk or hand blender, slowly drizzle the oil into the vinegar base. Thin it with a touch of water if the dressing gets too thick.

BLANCHED PEAS WITH MINT, RICOTTA, AND TOASTED WALNUTS

I have a massive love of springtime thanks to my upbringing in England, where the winters are long, wet, dark, cold, wet, gray, dreary—and did I mention wet? But all that horrible winter damp and mist makes Britain a gloriously green place in the spring and summer, full of colorful local produce to cook with. Peas, even though they're a pain in the ass to shell, have always been a favorite of mine.

The thing about peas is that they have a very short growing season, and all of their sweetness turns to mealy, bland starch within a couple days of being picked. This means that unless you can locate very fresh spring peas from a good farmers' market or home garden, you're actually best buying frozen ones. They are flash-frozen at their peak and therefore tend to be of a better quality, frankly, than all but the freshest spring peas.

SERVES 4 TO 6

1½ cups fresh or frozen English peas

4 ounces walnuts, preferably whole

8 fresh mint leaves

2 shallots, finely chopped

Small handful of fresh cilantro leaves, chopped

Sea salt and freshly ground black pepper

3 to 4 tablespoons Balsamic Vinaigrette (page 126)

8 ounces Homemade Ricotta (page 62)

6 to 8 slices Ciabatta (page 49, or store-bought), toasted

1. Preheat the oven to 325°F.

2. If you're using fresh peas, bring a medium pot full of seawater-salty water to a boil and toss the peas in. Boil them for 6 to 8 minutes, then drain off the hot water and immediately transfer them to a bowl full of ice water to cool. If you're using frozen peas, allow them to thaw under cold running water.

3. Spread the walnuts evenly on a baking sheet, place them in the oven, and toast until golden and fragrant, about 5 minutes, tossing them once to help them toast evenly. Transfer them to a plate to cool. Meanwhile, slice the mint into thin strips (this is called julienning).

4. Chuck the peas, walnuts, shallots, mint, and cilantro into a bowl and season with salt and pepper. Drizzle on as much vinaigrette as you like and toss the mixture to coat.

5. Transfer the pea salad to a serving bowl or platter and dollop the ricotta on top. Serve with ciabatta on the side.

ROASTED BABY ARTICHOKES WITH BACON AND BALSAMIC VINEGAR

For the past fifteen years or so, it seems like every restaurant in the western hemisphere has had Brussels sprouts, bacon, and balsamic vinegar on its menu, and I'm guilty of it too. But it's with good reason: the dish is seriously tasty. When I opened my new Hollywood restaurant, Birch, I wanted to do something equally as delicious but a little bit different. So I substituted baby artichokes, in season in the spring and summer, to freshen up a wintery dish for the warmer months. Baby artichokes have the same earthiness as Brussels sprouts, but with a unique, sweet nuttiness too.

SERVES 4 TO 6

9 baby artichokes
(about 2 pounds)

2 lemons, cut in half

8 ounces thick-cut bacon,
cut into ½-inch lardons

1 teaspoon chopped
fresh rosemary

2 garlic cloves,
finely chopped

Kosher salt

3 tablespoons good-
quality balsamic vinegar

¼ cup extra-virgin olive oil

¼ teaspoon flaky sea
salt, such as Maldon

¼ teaspoon cracked
black pepper

1. Prep each artichoke by removing the tough outer leaves and peeling the outer layer from the stem with a vegetable peeler or a paring knife. Cut off the top third of the artichoke to remove the tough ends of the leaves. Cut them in half lengthwise and give them a rub all over with one of the lemons as you work so they don't oxidize and turn an unappealing brown color.

2. Preheat the oven to 375°F.

3. Place a skillet big enough to fit the artichokes in a single layer over medium heat. Add the bacon lardons and cook for 5 minutes, or until most of their fat has been rendered. Remove the bacon using a slotted spoon and set it aside on a plate.

4. Add the artichokes to the hot bacon fat in a single layer and let them brown, about 3 minutes. Transfer the pan to the oven and cook for 10 minutes, or until soft and tender.

5. Remove the pan from the oven and add the bacon back in, along with the rosemary and garlic. Return the pan to a burner over medium heat. Give your best go at sautéing, tossing the ingredients around; if you drop some, don't worry, the dog will love you for it. Season with salt.

6. Add the vinegar to deglaze the pan, scraping up any browned bits with a wooden spoon, and let the vinegar reduce until sticky but not burnt, about 1 minute.

7. Transfer the artichokes and bacon to a serving bowl, drizzle with the oil, and sprinkle with sea salt and pepper.

ROASTED WINTER VEGETABLE AND BURRATA SALAD

The idea of a warm salad sounds a bit daft, but the contrast of temperatures at play here is really quite delicious. This salad is all about a balance of diverse flavors and textures. The rich nuts and cheese along with the sweet root vegetables make it quite substantial and filling as salads go.

SERVES 4 TO 6

4 ounces hazelnuts

1 small parsnip

1 carrot

2 small turnips

4 small shallots

Sea salt and freshly ground black pepper

½ cup good-quality extra-virgin olive oil, plus a bit more for the vegetables

¼ cup honey, preferably sage blossom honey

1 tablespoon Dijon mustard

¼ cup aged sherry vinegar

1 cup grapeseed oil

1 yellow endive

1 red endive

4 (4-ounce) balls burrata cheese

1. Preheat the oven to 325°F.

2. Spread the hazelnuts evenly on a baking sheet and toast them until golden brown and extremely fragrant, about 5 minutes. Crush them up a bit and set them aside.

3. Peel the parsnip, carrot, turnips, and shallots and cut them into bite-sized, roughly uniform pieces. Toss them in a bowl with salt, pepper, and a touch of olive oil, then spread them evenly on a baking sheet and roast until soft and caramelized, about 25 minutes. Allow them to cool slightly.

4. While your vegetables are cooking, prepare the vinaigrette by whisking the honey, mustard, and vinegar in a medium bowl. Add ½ teaspoon salt and 5 turns of the peppermill. Slowly whisk in the grapeseed oil and the remaining olive oil.

5. In a large bowl, separate the endive leaves and discard the cores. Add the roasted vegetables and half of the hazelnuts. Drizzle on as much vinaigrette as you like and toss to dress.

6. Divide the salad among plates or arrange it on a large platter. Break up the balls of burrata and distribute them across the top of the salad. Sprinkle the remaining hazelnuts on top and serve.

BEETS FROM A PRESSURE COOKER

I started cooking beets in a pressure cooker because I noticed that with light-colored varieties like golden beets or candy-striped Chioggias, roasting them in the oven altered their color for the worse. In a pressure cooker, not only do they keep their bright appearance, but they also cook much more quickly and keep their integrity better. So this one's a no-brainer.

SERVES 2

1 bunch beets (red, golden, or Chioggia), scrubbed and tops removed

3 tablespoons extra-virgin olive oil, plus more for finishing

Kosher salt and freshly ground black pepper

4 cups water

1. Place the cleaned beets in a small bowl, toss them with the oil, and season with salt and pepper.

2. Pour the water into your pressure cooker, insert a steamer tray, and place the dressed beets on top.

3. Close and lock the pressure cooker according to the manufacturer's instructions. Bring it to high pressure and cook the beets for 30 minutes. Depressurize the cooker and remove the beets. Allow them to cool, and then using a paper towel or a paring knife, carefully peel off the skin.

4. Cut the beets into segments and dress them with some more oil, salt, and pepper. Serve at room temperature.

SUNCHOKE SOUP

Sunchokes—also knows as Jerusalem artichokes—have a sweet and nutty flavor that's unique in the vegetable world. At one of my first jobs, at a very famous restaurant in London, we made croquettes with sunchokes and I forgot to order them as part of our vegetable delivery. The sous chef, who I think wanted to fire me anyway, tossed me out on the street and told me to come back with sunchokes—not as easy to find in London in the 90s—or lose my job. I spent hours walking around with the fear of God in me, and just when I'd almost given up, I stumbled across some at a market. Needless to say, I had a huge "Go F yourself!" smile on my face when I handed them over.

These little tubers are just now gaining the popularity they deserve among chefs, who thanks to today's emphasis on cooking with the seasons find themselves scratching around for new and interesting flavors on their winter menus. Sunchokes are often served roasted, but I like them pureed smooth into soup and garnished with mushrooms (for umami) and smoked almonds (for texture).

SERVES 6

½ cup extra-virgin olive oil, plus more for drizzling

2 garlic cloves, minced

1 teaspoon fresh thyme leaves, plus more for garnish

1½ pounds sunchokes, peeled and chopped

3 to 4 cups chicken stock

1 teaspoon kosher salt

¼ teaspoon freshly ground pepper

6 ounces chanterelle mushrooms

2 teaspoons fresh lemon juice

5 tablespoons crème fraîche, optional

¼ cup chopped smoked almonds

1. In a medium saucepan over medium heat, heat 2 tablespoons of the oil until it shimmers. Add the garlic and thyme and cook, stirring, for 1 minute.

2. Add the sunchokes, 3 cups of the chicken stock, ¼ cup of the remaining oil, the salt, and pepper. Bring the liquid to a simmer and cover the pan. Reduce the heat to low and cook for 30 minutes, or until the sunchokes are soft and are practically falling apart. If some of the tubers refuse to fall apart, cut them into smaller chunks with a knife (if you're in a terrible hurry, you can do this step in a pressure cooker at high pressure for 8 to 10 minutes).

3. Meanwhile, heat the last 2 tablespoons of oil in a medium sauté pan over medium heat until it shimmers. Add the chanterelles and cook until golden, 4 to 5 minutes. Set them aside.

4. Dump the soup into a blender and puree it until silky smooth, adding up to an additional cup of chicken stock to get it to your preferred texture. Stir in the lemon juice and half of the crème fraîche, if using.

5. Ladle the soup into bowls and top with the sautéed chanterelles, smoked almonds, some thyme leaves, the remaining crème fraîche, and a drizzle of oil.

CAULIFLOWER THREE WAYS

Kale and Brussels sprouts might be the trendy vegetables du jour, but for me it doesn't get any better than plain old horrendously unfashionable cauliflower. I fell in love with it when I went to see my grandma as a small child, and she cooked a dish that we Brits call cauliflower cheese: a gratin of sorts that she made with the best British cheddar and cauliflower that granddad grew in his garden.

Cauliflower is incredibly versatile, holds up to strong flavors, and it's really inexpensive for the quantity of food you get out of it. You can get specimens of a reasonably good quality all over the place, not just in fancy grocery stores and farmers' markets. Here are three of my favorite uses for dear old cauliflower, but simply boiled with a bit of salt and butter works just fine too.

SERVES 4

ROASTED WHOLE

½ cup (1 stick) salted butter

1 head cauliflower, green stalks
and outer leaves removed

½ teaspoon cumin seeds 1 whole garlic clove

1 sprig thyme

1 sprig rosemary

Sea salt and freshly ground black pepper

½ lemon

1. Preheat the oven to 350°F.

2. Grab a medium cast-iron pan and melt half of the butter over medium-high heat. Add the cauliflower and let it caramelize all over, adjusting it as necessary so that all of its surfaces color evenly without burning. Remove the cauliflower from the pan and add the remaining butter, the cumin seeds, garlic, and herbs, spooning them evenly around the surface of the pan.

3. Add the cauliflower back to the pan and spoon the butter over the top a few times. Transfer to the oven and cook for 15 minutes, basting it with the butter every 3 to 4 minutes (or as often as you can be bothered).

4. Remove the cauliflower from the oven and give it one last butter baste. Sprinkle it with salt, pepper, and lemon juice. Cut it into wedges and serve.

(continued)

SOUP

SERVES 4

6 tablespoons unsalted butter

½ yellow onion, sliced

2 garlic cloves, minced

¼ teaspoon ground cumin

1 small head cauliflower, green stalks and outer leaves removed, coarsely chopped

Kosher salt

2 cups chicken or vegetable stock

½ cup heavy cream

Freshly ground black pepper

3 ounces Parmesan, grated

1. Place a 6-quart saucepan or Dutch oven over medium-high heat and melt the butter. Turn down the heat to medium-low and add the onion and garlic. Cook until the onions become translucent and begin to smell sweet, 6 to 7 minutes.

2. Stir in the cumin and cook for a minute or two. Chuck in the cauliflower and a big pinch of salt and cook for a further 3 minutes.

3. Add the stock and jack up the heat to bring it to a boil. Reduce the heat to keep the soup at a simmer for 5 to 7 minutes. Add the cream and simmer for 3 minutes more.

4. Using a food processor, standing blender, or, better yet, an immersion blender, puree the soup until it's smooth as a baby's bottom. Taste and add more salt if necessary. Reheat the soup and serve it sprinkled with freshly ground black pepper and Parmesan.

"T-BONE" STEAKS

SERVES 4

1 medium to large head cauliflower,
green stalks and outer leaves removed

Splash of canola oil

Kosher salt and freshly ground black pepper

4 to 6 ounces blue cheese, crumbled

4 tablespoons Herb Butter (page 35)

1 cup bread crumbs

1 tablespoon chopped fresh parsley

1. Preheat the oven to 350°F.

2. Place the cauliflower stem-end down on your
   cutting board and slice off the rounded ends
   on the right and left-hand sides. Slice it into
   4 cross-sections of even thickness.

3. Heat a cast-iron skillet over medium-high heat and
   add a splash of oil. Season the cauliflower steaks
   with salt. Unless you have a flipping huge pan or a
   very small cauliflower, this probably will require
   working in batches or using two pans: sear the
   steaks on one side for 3 to 4 minutes, until golden
   brown. Flip them and spread crumbled blue
   cheese and bits of the herb butter as evenly as
   possible on top. Sprinkle with bread crumbs.

4. Transfer the pan to the oven and cook until the
   cauliflower is tender, the butter and cheese are
   melted, and bread crumbs are golden and crisp,
   5 to 10 minutes. Repeat step 3 with the remaining
   cauliflower steaks as necessary. Sprinkle with
   freshly ground black pepper and parsley and serve.

THREE POTATO RECIPES

Growing up in England in the 1980s, pasta, rice, and certainly any sort of Asian noodle or grains like quinoa or farro were seriously edgy stuff. I was raised on potatoes; ate them with practically every meal. A nice creamy mash or a stack of crispy chips to this day reminds me of the comforts of home.

When it comes to cooking potatoes, it's all about honing and perfecting a few versatile methods rather than trying out a bunch of crazy recipes; keep the potatoes uncomplicated and look to your veggies for newness and variation. The following recipes relay my tried-and-tested techniques to boil, mash, and fry potatoes—the only three preparations you need in order to round out any dinner plate, any time of the year.

PLAIN BOILED POTATOES

Beginner cooks have a nasty habit of either undercooking boiled potatoes or severely overcooking them. Undercooked spuds are crunchy and therefore more or less inedible, and when overcooked, they get waterlogged and taste of nothing. The key to getting them just right is timing, not water temperature. Let them boil away, then take them off the heat once a knife slides through the potatoes without any resistance, like a hot knife through butter. If the water becomes floury and the potatoes start to break apart, you've overcooked them. Start over.

Don't let the use of mint in this recipe throw you off. It has the effect of slightly sweetening the potatoes but won't leave them tasting like toothpaste or chewing gum.

SERVES 2

1 pound fingerling potatoes
1 teaspoon kosher salt
3 sprigs mint
1 sprig thyme
8 black peppercorns
Salted butter or Whipped Lardo (page 59) for serving

1. Give your potatoes a good scrub, put them in a large saucepan, and cover them with water by at least an inch. Add the salt and stir. Bring the water to a boil and add the mint, thyme, and peppercorns.

2. Boil the potatoes until tender, 15 to 25 minutes, depending on their size. Turn off the heat and leave the potatoes to cool in the water. This will allow them to soak up the flavor of the herbs and pepper and keep them from steaming themselves dry.

3. Drain the potatoes and serve them with a knob of butter or perhaps a dollop of whipped lardo (especially if they're going with pork).

THE MOST EXCELLENT MASHED POTATOES

A great mashed potato recipe is one of the best things a man can learn. They go with nearly anything, and good-quality potatoes are easy to find wherever you are in the world. My ideal mashed potatoes are glossy, custardy, and contain almost as much butter as potato (sorry, but they're not a diet food). I like to use Yukon gold potatoes, because they have a buttery richness to them and don't absorb a lot of water when cooking.

Pick out potatoes that are even in size and don't have too many eyes (which are a sign that they're really old). If they've been sitting in your kitchen pantry for a while, make sure they're still firm with a sweet—never musty—smell to them. Keep in mind that mashed potatoes don't make good leftovers, so cook only what you'll eat in one sitting. They absorb moisture and take on off flavors in the fridge, and once cooled and reheated, they'll never have the same texture again.

Salt

1 pound large fingerling or Yukon gold potatoes, peeled (and cut into quarters, if using Yukon gold)

About 1 pound (4 sticks) unsalted butter

About ½ cup organic whole milk

1. Bring 2 quarts of water with 1 tablespoon salt to a boil over high heat. Add the potatoes and cook for 12 to 15 minutes, until a paring knife easily inserts and removes from the potatoes.

2. Turn the heat to low. Drain the potatoes well and return them to the pan for a minute or two to evaporate any excess water, stirring them constantly. Put the potatoes through a potato ricer.

3. In the same pan set over medium heat, melt 3 sticks of butter and add ¼ cup milk. Add the potatoes and a pinch of salt and whisk the mixture together, continuing to add milk until the potatoes take on an almost custard-like consistency. At this stage, you can add more butter and salt to suit your taste, but it's important to maintain the earthy flavor of the potatoes—so don't get too greedy with the butter.

(continued)

TRIPLE-COOKED CHIPS

"Chips" in England are what you call "fries" here in America (to confuse matters further, your "chips" are our "crisps"). Regardless of what the hell you call them, chips, crisps, hash browns, French fries, home fries, patatas bravas—fried potatoes of all sorts might be the most consumed snack in the Western world. My feeling is that if you're going to down this much fat and salt, they'd better be proper worth it. That's why I make the chips in-house at my restaurant instead of buying in the frozen kind, much as my overworked cooks would probably prefer to do the latter and save themselves a couple hours on spud duty every morning. Boiled, oven-dried, and twice fried, these chips end up with a mashed-potato-soft interior and a fried crust so sturdy that they crunch when you eat them.

SERVES 4

2 pounds Kennebec or russet potatoes
Table salt
Canola oil for frying

1. Scrub the potatoes under cold water. Using a sharp knife, square off their round edges slightly, then slice them into ½-inch × ½-inch fry shapes.

2. Preheat the oven to 375°F.

3. Chuck the fries in a pot and cover them with cold, seawater-salty water by at least an inch. Bring the water to a simmer over medium-high heat; it's important to always start potatoes cooking in cold water and heat them gradually, which allows them to release starch and prevents them from becoming gummy. Leave the potatoes to cook all the way through, 5 or so minutes after the water begins to simmer.

4. Line 2 baking sheets with parchment paper. Gently remove the potatoes from the hot water to one of the sheets and place them in the oven for 2 minutes to dry—this will help them crisp in the fryer and develop a really crunchy outside shell.

5. If you've got an electric fryer by chance, use it, because they're way safer; if not, take a heavy pot like a Dutch oven and fill it half full with oil. Position a thermometer in the oil and heat it nice and slow over medium heat until the temperature reads 300°F.

6. Transfer the potatoes to the fryer in batches and fry them until pale golden, about 2 minutes. Remove them from the fryer with a slotted spoon or skimmer to the second parchment-lined baking sheet and place them back in the oven for 2 minutes more. At this point, the fries can be cooled and stored in a sealed container in the fridge for a day or two.

7. Increase the oil temperature to 375°F and return the fries to the fryer once more, again working in batches. This time, cook them until deep golden and very crisp, 2 to 3 minutes. Transfer them to paper towels and immediately hit them with salt. Serve immediately.

SPECIAL DAYS

A SUMMER COOKOUT

SPINACH AND ARTICHOKE DIP

LAMB BELLY WITH MINT SAUCE

CORN ON THE COB WITH CHILE-LIME BUTTER

LAMBURGERS

ROOT VEGETABLES

SWORDFISH WITH SALSA VERDE

CHICKEN AL MATTONE

THE GRILLING RECIPES THAT I REGULARLY COME ACROSS IN COOKBOOKS are unbelievably one-dimensional and boring; basically, endless repetitions of the same steak and hamburger cuisine. Rather than pile on a few more, I thought I'd show you lads what your grills can really do. Think lamb belly and swordfish, not burgers and weenies. Pick and choose from the recipes in this chapter to create whatever sort of cookout style suits your fancy.

SPINACH AND ARTICHOKE DIP

I know I've put artichokes in the title of this book, but if I'm being honest, I had never seen one never mind eaten one until I was nineteen, and my first impression was, "That's a lot of messing about for something so bland!" I still think they're a pain in the ass to prepare, but in season and with a lot of love, I now appreciate that artichokes are absolutely delicious and just about worth all the effort. I would recommend steering clear of the prepared canned ones, tempting as they are, because they are flavorless and sometimes have a woody texture.

I wanted to include a recipe for artichoke dip for a couple of reasons: first, because Yanks love dips. Second, because I think that other than being served with bacon and Balsamic Vinaigrette (page 126), this is the absolute best way to eat them.

SERVES 6

4 medium globe artichokes

1 whole garlic clove

1 slice lemon

1 bay leaf

2 tablespoons extra-virgin olive oil

Salt

3 garlic cloves, minced

2½ cups fresh baby spinach, chopped

1 cup ricotta cheese

8 ounces cream cheese

1 teaspoon chile flakes

1 tablespoon tahini

Freshly ground black pepper

½ cup grated Parmesan

Fresh lemon juice

Pita Bread (page 157) for serving, optional

1. Using a serrated knife, cut ¾ to 1 inch off the top of an artichoke. Pull off the scabby, smaller leaves toward the base and on the stem. Cut the stem back to 1 inch in length. Repeat with the remaining artichokes.

2. Fill a large pot with 2 inches of water and add the whole garlic clove, the lemon slice, bay leaf, and a good pinch of salt. Add the artichokes in a single layer and cover the pot. Bring the liquid to a boil over medium-high heat, then reduce the heat to a simmer. Cover and cook the artichokes until the outer leaves can easily be pulled off, 35 to 45 minutes.

3. Remove the artichokes from the pot and, once they are cool enough to handle, pull off all the tough outer leaves. Using a spoon, scrape out and discard the inedible fuzzy bit in the middle of the artichoke (it's known as the choke, for good reason: that's what it would make you do if you ate the bloody stuff!). You will be left with artichoke hearts; cut these into ½-inch slices (you should have about 1 cup).

4. Preheat the oven to 350°F.

5. Heat the oil in a large skillet over medium heat. Add the minced garlic, followed by the spinach, and cook until the spinach is wilted but still bright green, 2 to 4 minutes. Remove the pan from the heat and stir in the ricotta cheese and cream cheese, mixing well. Add the sliced artichoke hearts. Stir in the chile flakes and tahini and season with salt and pepper. Add half of the Parmesan cheese and lemon juice to taste. Mix well.

6. Spread the mixture into a 1-quart baking dish. Sprinkle the remaining Parmesan on top.

7. Bake the dip in the center of the oven for 15 minutes. Turn on the broiler and broil until the cheese has melted and the top is bubbly with lightly browned edges. This will only take a minute or so, so watch carefully and don't bloody burn it. Serve hot, with pita bread if you like.

LAMB BELLY WITH MINT SAUCE

In the ten years that I've been cooking in the States, I've watched the popularity of lamb grow tremendously. That's a hardship for a lamb lover like me, believe it or not, because it means that prices have gone through the roof for choice bits like chops and roasts. Luckily for me there is plenty of deliciousness to be found in cheap cuts of meat, such as shanks and bellies.

Lamb belly is well-marbled with fat and has loads of flavor when cooked correctly. That means rendering—or liquefying—the big strips of fat running through the meat so that you don't end up with a mouthful of solid lard. In this recipe, the lamb belly cooks slowly in a sealed packet, allowing all that lovely fat to render down and baste the meat. You're left with a thin sheet of very tender, almost confit belly meat. We finish it on the grill for a hint of that bitter, smoky flavor of char and serve it with a sweet-and-sour mint sauce, both of which balance out the lovely fattiness.

SERVES 4 TO 6

2 (1- to 1½-pound) lamb bellies

Kosher salt and freshly ground black pepper

½ teaspoon chopped fresh thyme

½ teaspoon chopped fresh rosemary

3 tablespoons malt vinegar

1 tablespoon light brown sugar

5 tablespoons chopped fresh mint

1. Preheat the oven to 300°F.

2. Trim the lamb bellies of excess fat and sinew and season them with salt, pepper, and the thyme and rosemary.

3. Pull a piece of plastic wrap out onto a clean work surface, press the two lamb bellies together, and roll them in plastic no fewer than 2 to 3 times, keeping the bellies as flat as possible. Turn the bellies 180 degrees and wrap them in 2 to 3 more layers of plastic. Now repeat the process using aluminum foil.

4. Place the lamb belly package in a large roasting pan and pour hot water in to reach halfway up the bellies. Place the roasting pan on the stovetop and bring the water to a boil over high heat. Carefully transfer the pan to the oven and cook it for 3 hours, topping off the water as necessary to keep it at around the same level. Transfer it from oven and allow it to rest for 1 hour. Unwrap the meat once it's cool enough to handle, or transfer it still wrapped to the refrigerator, where it will keep for up to 4 days.

5. Meanwhile, place the vinegar and brown sugar in a small pan and warm it over medium heat, stirring until the sugar dissolves. Remove the pan from the heat and allow it to cool. Stir in the mint and let it marinate.

6. Prepare your grill for medium-high-heat cooking. Grill the lamb bellies for 2 to 3 minutes per side. Transfer them to a platter or cutting board, spoon the mint sauce over the top, and serve.

CORN ON THE COB WITH CHILE-LIME BUTTER

As good as simple steamed corn on the cob can be, the roasty, rich, charred flavor you get by cooking it over dry heat is truly unbeatable. The most common way to do this is to put the corn on the grill, but you can follow the same method using a 475°F oven instead. Just cook the corn cobs on top of a baking sheet that's been preheated along with the oven.

If the powdered milk is weirding you out, give me the benefit of the doubt. It adds some cheesy sweetness to balance the hot and sour butter, as well as a little bit of crunchy texture. All in all, the dish is a spin on *elotes*, the grilled corn covered in cheese that's a common Mexican street food.

SERVES 8

½ cup (1 stick) unsalted butter, at room temperature

1 canned chipotle chile in adobo, finely chopped

1 tablespoon freshly grated lime zest

1½ tablespoons kosher salt, plus more for seasoning

1½ tablespoons Maldon sea salt or fleur de sel

1½ tablespoons Maldon smoked salt

1 teaspoon hot smoked paprika

1 tablespoon coarsely ground black pepper

⅓ cup powdered milk

8 ears corn, shucked

Vegetable oil for drizzling

1. Place the butter on a cutting board and sprinkle it with the minced chipotle, lime zest, and a little kosher salt. Using a knife, finely chop the ingredients together until they're well-combined. Transfer the butter mixture to a sheet of parchment paper, wax paper, or plastic wrap. Fold the paper over and roll it into a cylinder, twisting the ends. Wrap that airtight in foil, then chill the butter until solid. It will keep refrigerated for up to 2 weeks or frozen for up to 3 months.

2. Fire up your gas or charcoal grill as hot as it will go. Mix together the three salts, the paprika, and black pepper in a small bowl and set it aside.

3. In a small skillet over medium heat, toast off the milk powder until golden brown, 3 to 5 minutes, tossing it constantly to avoid burning. Set aside.

4. Drizzle the corn cobs with oil, rubbing to coat each ear thoroughly. Place them on the grill's cooking grate, turning them often, until the corn is lightly charred all over and just tender, about 15 minutes. Transfer the corn to a large platter and serve it with the lime chipotle butter, seasoned salts, and caramelized milk powder on the side. Job done.

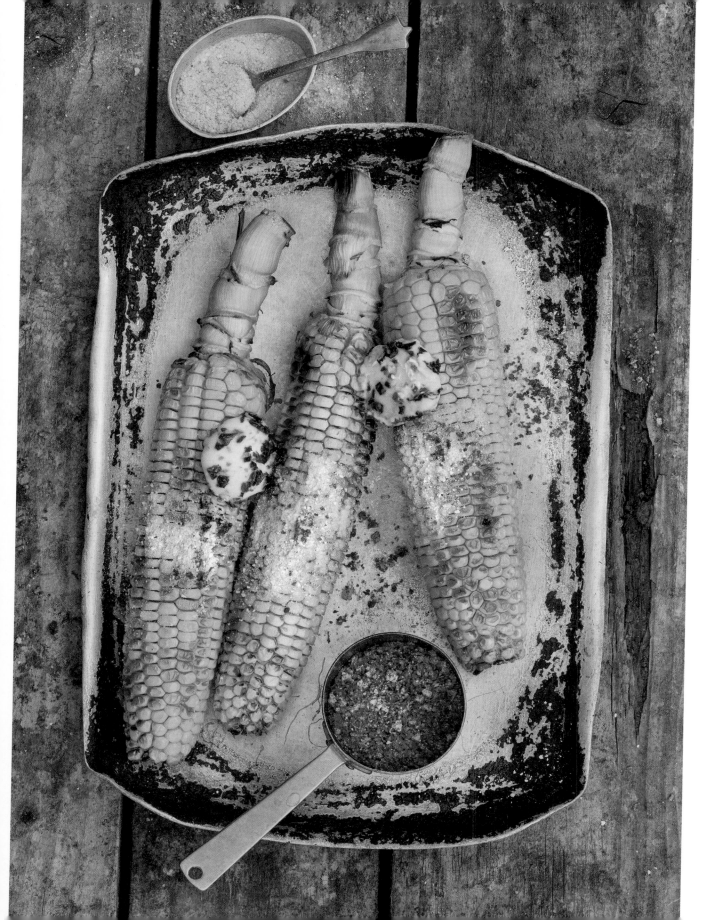

LAMBURGERS

What it is it about men and beef? People can't seem to stop themselves from giving chaps recipe upon recipe for hamburgers and steak, even though neither is really all that complicated. I figured that if I was going to show you yet another burger, it ought to be made from lamb.

I love lamb in general and find that it's exceptionally good in burger format. Just ask the Turks; their *doner* kebabs are basically little lamburgers on sticks. The fattiness of ground lamb makes for incredibly juicy burgers, with the kind of flavor you could only get from beef by grinding up a dry-aged porterhouse. I've kitted these out with my favorite toppings—mushrooms, Gruyère cheese, onion marmalade, arugula, and a pickly, hot, minty yogurt sauce that puts Big Mac sauce to shame— but you can top them with whatever you please. Make sure to use a sturdy bun, which can stand up to the profusion of juices that will come from the meat. And of course, if you don't care for lamb, you can always substitute ground beef and make these regular old hamburgers.

SERVES 4

1 tablespoon
unsalted butter

1 cup sliced white
mushrooms

2 pounds ground lamb,
preferably 80% lean
Colorado lamb

Salt

4 tablespoons Caramelized
Onion Compote (page 21)

4 slices Gruyère or
Swiss cheese

4 burger buns, preferably
Martin's Potato Rolls or
King's Hawaiian Rolls

1 cup arugula

Freshly ground
black pepper

Olive oil for drizzling

4 tablespoons Special
Sauce (recipe follows)

1. Heat the butter in a cast-iron pan over medium-high heat until it melts and begins to foam. Add the mushrooms and cook until soft and golden, 4 to 5 minutes. Set aside.

2. Prepare your grill for medium-high-heat cooking.

3. Divide your lamb into four 8-ounce portions. Season them generously with salt and roll each into a ball. Wrap the balls tightly in plastic wrap and then flatten them with the heel of your hand into patties about 5 inches in diameter and ½-inch thick; the plastic will help mold and pack the meat. Use your thumb to make a dimple in the center of the patty (this helps the burger keep its shape as it cooks). Remove the plastic wrap.

4. Gently place the burgers on the grill over direct heat. Resist the urge to mash them into the grate with a spatula, which does nothing to help them cook nicely. Leave them alone for 3 minutes for medium-rare; add a minute or two for a better-cooked burger. Flip them, and after 2 minutes, top each with the onion compote, mushrooms, and cheese. Cook the burgers for a minute more, then transfer them to a platter or baking sheet. They should measure 125°F for medium-rare, 135°F for medium.

5. Place the buns on the grill cut-side down for a minute or two to warm them. In a small bowl, dress the arugula with salt, pepper, and a bit of oil.

6. Spread the bottom of each bun with special sauce, then transfer the burgers to their buns. Top them with the arugula, close with a bun, and serve.

(continued)

SPECIAL SAUCE

MAKES ¾ CUP

½ cup Greek yogurt

1 tablespoon diced roasted red peppers

1 tablespoon diced cornichons

1 tablespoon diced capers

1½ teaspoons fresh lemon juice

1½ teaspoons harissa paste or harissa powder

1 tablespoon chopped fresh mint

1 tablespoon chopped fresh cilantro

Kosher salt and freshly ground black pepper

Chuck all the ingredients in a small bowl, mix them well, and season the sauce with salt and pepper.

GIVE IT SOME GAS

Chefs tend to go absolutely mental on the subject of charcoal grilling and its superiority to grilling with propane gas. Charcoal's flavor is the whole point, they'll argue, and there's an art to managing the heat of a live fire. Gas grilling, with its push-button ignition and temperature-altering knobs, is for amateurs.

Call me a sell-out, but while gas grilling may be a little lacking in the romance department, it's also about a thousand times more convenient than mucking about with charcoal on your average weeknight. With a charcoal grill, there is the stacking and lighting of the coals to manage and the wait for them to turn ready for cooking; with gas, you flick a switch and go. Since a charcoal fire burns hot for hours, it would be madness to get the grill going for a single piece of fish; gas, on the other hand, goes off and on instantly. I won't deny that charcoal lends its own delicious flavor to food, but insisting on charcoal is letting the perfect be the enemy of the good.

There's also a common misconception that if you buy a gas grill, it needs to be big and tricked out to do the job right. The truth is, even those little piece of shit grills with portable propane canisters are perfectly all right to use.

There is good reason to make grilling as easy as possible. It's super healthy, since you use no cooking fat and the grilling process actually drains fat away from meats. Cooking directly over a flame, even a gas flame, produces a beautiful flavor of char that isn't easy to achieve in the oven or on the stove. And getting a breath of fresh air while you make dinner is a nice bonus of its own, wouldn't you say?

ROOT VEGETABLES

Root vegetables might not be the first thing that comes to mind when you think about grilling—most people go straight to summer produce like zucchini, eggplant, and peppers. But the abundant natural sugars in carrots, parsnips, turnips, and the like react beautifully to the dry heat of the grill, caramelizing, intensifying, and charring.

A note about the oil you use: I call for blended oil here, which you'll see on the grocery store shelf as a blend of about 75 percent vegetable oil and 25 percent olive oil. Try to avoid pure olive oil, which can lend a bitter taste when heated to high temperatures.

SERVES 4 TO 6

2 carrots, peeled and split

2 parsnips, peeled and split

1 celery root, peeled and cut into ½-inch planks

2 small fennel bulbs, split

1 rutabaga, peeled and cut into ½-inch planks

1 turnip, peeled and cut into ½-inch planks

¼ cup blended vegetable oil

Kosher salt and freshly ground black pepper

½ cup (1 stick) unsalted butter

Zest of 1 lemon

1 tablespoon finely chopped *fines herbes* (parsley, chives, tarragon, and chervil)

1. Prepare the grill for medium-high-heat cooking.

2. In a large bowl, toss all of the vegetables in the oil with a generous sprinkling of salt and a few grinds of pepper.

3. Place the vegetables on the grill, avoiding any hot spots. Grill the vegetables on all sides until cooked through and tender, 7 to 10 minutes. Remove them from the grill.

4. Place a small saucepan on the grill and melt your butter in it.

5. In a large bowl, toss the grilled vegetables, melted butter, lemon zest, and *fines herbes*. Taste and add salt as needed. Arrange the veggies on a big platter and serve.

SWORDFISH WITH SALSA VERDE

I had never tried swordfish until I moved to the States, and even then it wasn't until I watched the movie *The Perfect Storm* and had to see what all the fuss was about. It turns out that fresh-caught swordfish really is good enough to risk life and limb over. It's meaty in both flavor and texture, so if you're not much of a fish eater, this is a great place to start. You might remember that back in the 90s Atlantic swordfish was being overfished and therefore wasn't a responsible species to eat. Now, thanks to good fishery management, swordfish populations are back on solid footing and it's a perfectly sustainable seafood option.

SERVES 4

¼ cup salted capers, soaked for 30 minutes, drained, and coarsely chopped

½ cup chopped fresh flat-leaf parsley

⅓ cup chopped scallions, white and green parts

½ cup chopped fresh mint leaves

½ cup plus 2 tablespoons fresh lemon juice

2 teaspoons grated lemon zest

1 cup plus 2 tablespoons extra-virgin olive oil

2 teaspoons chile flakes

Kosher salt

1½ teaspoons freshly ground black pepper

4 (6-ounce) swordfish steaks, ¾-inch thick

1. Chuck the capers, parsley, scallions, mint, ½ cup of the lemon juice, the lemon zest, 1 cup oil, and 1 teaspoon of the chile flakes in the jug of a blender. Puree them until smooth, season with salt, and set aside.

2. Prepare the grill for medium-high-heat cooking. Mix together the remaining 2 tablespoons lemon juice and remaining 2 tablespoons of the oil. Brush the swordfish steaks on both sides with the lemon-oil mixture and season them with salt, pepper, and the remaining 1 teaspoon chile flakes.

3. Grill the steaks until just cooked through, 3 to 4 minutes per side, and transfer them to plates. Spoon the salsa verde over the top and serve them with Plain Boiled Potatoes (page 138) and Butter Lettuce Salad (page 121).

CHICKEN AL MATTONE

I've had a thing for Italian food since I was a very young boy. My aunt was from Italy, and at her house I was exposed to really good homemade pasta, gnocchi, mortadella, and my favorite, Nutella. Her relatives would visit with all sorts of goodies, from salamis to prosciutto to Italian cheeses. It was probably little influences like these that subconsciously drew me to becoming a chef; that, and the fact that David Beckham was better at football than me, so I didn't get the call! And of course laying bricks just didn't have the same appeal.

Here is a dish of pure simplicity, using only a few ingredients and a very clever cooking technique—what we call "chicken under a brick" in England and America. Only the bloody Italians could come up with something this easy and tasty.

SERVES 3 TO 4

1 (3½- to 4-pound) organic chicken

4 tablespoons fresh lemon juice

3 tablespoons grapeseed or olive oil

1 tablespoon chopped fresh rosemary, plus additional sprigs for garnish

2 garlic cloves, pressed

Coarse salt and freshly ground black pepper

¼ teaspoon chile flakes

Chopped fresh flat-leaf parsley

1. Using a sharp chef's knife or a pair of poultry shears, cut the backbone out of the chicken so that the whole bird can be flattened into a single layer. This technique is called *spatchcock* (save the jokes for later, lads).

2. Place the chicken flat, skin-side down, on a baking sheet. Mix 2 tablespoons of the lemon juice, 2 tablespoons of the oil, the chopped rosemary, and garlic in a small bowl. Rub the mixture all over the chicken on both sides. Cover the chicken with plastic wrap and bang it in the fridge overnight.

3. Prepare your grill for low-heat cooking (around 250 to 275°F).

4. Brush the chicken with the remaining tablespoon of cooking oil and sprinkle it with salt and pepper. Put the chicken skin-side down on the grill, away from the flames.

5. Place a foil-wrapped brick (or cast-iron skillet) atop the chicken so that it sits perpendicular to the breastbone, keeping the chicken from buckling up. Grill the bird for 45 to 60 minutes (a general rule of thumb for chicken is about 18 to 20 minutes per pound).

6. Remove the brick and turn the chicken over, then put the brick back in place and continue to grill until juices run clear when thickest part of a thigh is pierced, 10 to 15 minutes longer.

7. Remove the brick and transfer the chicken to a plate. Drizzle it with the remaining 2 tablespoons lemon juice and sprinkle it with the chile flakes, some parsley, and rosemary.

GAME DAY

HOMEMADE PITA BREAD

SPICED LAMB SHANKS

SPICED YOGURT DIP

SWEET CHILI MARMALADE (PAGE 26)

INFUSED VINEGARS (PAGE 34)

MAYBE THE ESKIMOS ARE AN EXCEPTION, BUT MEN IN EVERY CULTURE, in every country around the world that I'm aware of, have the lads over from time to time to watch a game. In England, that game is football, rugby, or cricket, and it usually involves plenty of good, cold lagers and rib-sticking refreshments of some sort—often just chips and dips, but your better hosts will put together something a bit more inspired. For those occasions, here is a simple but delicious menu of fork-tender lamb shanks, homemade pita bread, and the necessary accompaniments—spiced yogurt dip, chili marmalade, and infused vinegars for dipping and dressing these lamb sandwiches. Better than fast-food pizza and wings, wouldn't you say?

HOMEMADE PITA BREAD

I read somewhere that it was our ability to farm wheat and make bread that changed the course of human history, giving birth to civilization. That certainly seems logical, as practically every nation and its people have their own form of bread that they make and eat. The pita comes from the Mediterranean and Middle East, which makes it one of the oldest forms of bread around.

Some breads are very complex to prepare, shape, and bake correctly, but pitas are quite rustic and straightforward. For this recipe, you'll need a small stand mixer or large triceps, plus a rolling pin, an oven, a bread stone (preferable) or two baking sheets (less ideal but OK). This recipe uses the "mother" method, which means that you first make a pre-fermentation starter before making the actual bread (see page 50 for more about bread mothers). It helps the bread rise (or "proof") well and lends it a really nice flavor profile.

MAKES 16 PITAS

1 teaspoon active dry yeast

2½ cups warm water (approximately 105°F)

2 cups whole wheat flour

About 4 cups bread flour

1 tablespoon salt

1 to 2 tablespoons olive oil

1. In the bowl of a stand mixer fitted with a dough hook attachment, combine the yeast and warm water. Turn the mixer on low speed just to stir the yeast mixture to help it dissolve.

2. Add the whole wheat flour, 1 cup at a time, followed by 1 cup of the bread flour. Mix the dough for 2 minutes to activate the gluten in the flour. Turn off the mixer, loosely cover the bowl with plastic wrap, and let it rest until it doubles in size, about 30 minutes.

3. Sprinkle the dough with salt and stir in the oil. Mix for 2 minutes. Add the rest of the bread flour, 1 cup at a time, and knead it with the dough hook on medium speed for 8 to 10 minutes, until the dough is elastic and pulls away from the bowl as one smooth mass.

4. Lightly oil the surface of the dough and cover it with plastic wrap. Let rise until at least double in size, approximately 1½ hours.

5. Turn the dough out onto a floured work surface and knock the air out of it with your hands. Portion out 16 eyeball-even balls and roll them out into circles approximately 8 to 9 inches in diameter and less than ¼-inch thick.

6. Preheat oven to 450°F and place a large baking stone or 2 baking sheets on a rack or racks toward the bottom of the oven.

7. Working in batches, bake the pitas for 5 minutes. Remove them from the oven and place them on a cooling rack for about 5 minutes to cool slightly, then wrap the breads in a large kitchen towel (this will keep them soft). Stuff and eat them immediately, or reheat them before use either in the oven or on a griddle.

SPICED LAMB SHANKS

I love shank meat of all sorts. It's got a lovely melt-in-your-mouth texture and a strong flavor of whatever beast you're eating, whether it's beef, veal, pork, or lamb. But this is a cut that you've got to cook low and slow, or else the meat will be tough as leather. I let these lamb shanks simmer away for hours in wine and stock flavored with warm spices, and the result is absolutely incredible. If you cook only one recipe from this book, it should be this. Wrapping the meat up in pita with a bit of yogurt sauce is ambrosia. Enjoy.

SERVES 4

1½ tablespoons olive oil

4 lamb shanks

3 onions, thinly sliced

4 garlic cloves, thinly sliced

½ cinnamon stick

2 star anise

1 tablespoon cumin
seeds, crushed

1 tablespoon coriander
seeds, crushed

Pinch of chile flakes

2 cups red wine

2 (15-ounce) cans
chopped tomatoes

4 ounces dates
(about 5 dates)

4 cups low-sodium
beef stock

2 tablespoons
pomegranate molasses

Salt

Handful of chopped
fresh cilantro

1. Preheat the oven to 300°F.

2. Place a Dutch oven big enough to hold the lamb shanks over medium-high heat and add the oil. Working in batches so as not to crowd the pot, caramelize the shanks, turning them every couple of minutes so they brown on all surfaces. Remove them from the pan and set them aside.

3. Turn the heat down to medium, add the onions to the pan, and cook until soft and translucent, about 10 minutes. Add the garlic and spices and cook for 4 minutes more. Add the wine and reduce it by two thirds, about 15 minutes. Chuck in the tomatoes, dates, and stock, then nestle the shanks back in on their sides so that they're mostly submerged in liquid. Bring the liquid to a boil, cover, and put it in the oven. Cook for 3 to 4 hours, until fork-tender.

4. Remove the lid and stir through the molasses. Pull out the shanks and wrap them in foil to keep them warm. Place the Dutch oven over medium heat, bring the cooking liquid to a simmer, and reduce it down until thick and glossy. Stir it regularly to keep the sauce together.

5. Taste the sauce and add salt as needed. Place the shanks on a big serving platter and pour the sauce over the top. Scatter with cilantro and serve. Or you can pull the meat off the bones, drizzle it with the Spiced Yogurt Dip (page 160), and serve in Homemade Pita Bread (page 157) for some tasty sandwiches.

SPICED YOGURT DIP

When you think "English chef," your mind probably goes to fish and chips, roast beef, and sticky toffee pudding. The truth is, I think the most eaten dish in England for the past twenty years has been chicken tikka masala! We Brits absolutely love Indian food, so it seemed only right to include at least one recipe from the subcontinent in this book. This cooling yogurt sauce is known as raita in Indian cuisine, and it's wonderful for taking the edge off spicy or rich foods.

MAKES 3 CUPS

1 English cucumber, thinly sliced

Kosher salt

2 cups whole milk yogurt (not the Greek variety)

½ cup finely chopped red onion

¼ cup coarsely chopped fresh cilantro

2 tablespoons fresh lime juice

¼ teaspoon ground coriander

¼ teaspoon ground cumin

⅛ teaspoon freshly ground black pepper

Tiny pinch of freshly grated nutmeg

Tiny pinch of ground cinnamon

Tiny pinch of ground cardamom

1. Place the cucumber slices in a colander and sprinkle them liberally with salt, tossing to combine. Let the cukes drain for 30 minutes, then rinse them with cold water. Place the cucumbers between paper towels for 5 minutes, pressing down from time to time to extract as much water as possible.

2. In a medium bowl, combine the cucumber slices with the remaining ingredients and season with salt.

CHRISTMAS

A CHRISTMAS PUNCH

CHICKEN LIVER PÂTÉ

A JOINT OF BEEF AND A PROPER GRAVY

TURNIP AND POTATO GRATIN

YORKSHIRE PUDDINGS

EGG NOG ICE CREAM

APPLE PIE

CHRISTMAS IS TYPICALLY A TIME OF YEAR WHEN WIVES AND MUMS ALWAYS have their hands full, and I've found it to be a good opportunity for the men of the family to step up, show their worth, and take charge of some of the festive food. It is also, in truth, a fantastic time to be on kitchen duty. Christmas feasting is all about rich and indulgent flavors, without any particular consideration for waistlines or wallets. A word to the wise: having a bowl of punch on the go means you'll have lots of company in the kitchen, which means extra hands for peeling, chopping, and mixing.

A CHRISTMAS PUNCH

In England we always drink punch at Christmas, so obviously I got hammered on the stuff when I was about eleven and didn't touch it again until well into my thirties. Now I'm old enough to fully appreciate how gathering around a punch bowl is a perfect fit for the festive, social nature of the holidays. It also frees the host up from mixing individual drinks to better focus on cooking, opening presents, and general merrymaking.

SERVES 8 TO 12

Peels from 3 lemons (ideally without any white pith)

18 white sugar cubes

18 strawberries, topped and sliced

3 wheels fresh pineapple, each cut into 8 pieces

1 tablespoon vanilla extract

12 ounces bourbon (I like Buffalo Trace)

6 ounces gin (any London dry will do)

18 ounces chilled soda water

1. In a medium bowl, combine the lemon peels and sugar. Mix them up and mash them with the back of a spoon (this is called *muddling*) to extract their oil. Leave the mixture for at least an hour or up to three hours, taking a crack at muddling the peels and sugar from time to time. Eventually a syrup will form from the sugar and lemon oil.

2. Add the strawberries, pineapple, and vanilla extract. Stir well and let sit for another hour.

3. Add the booze and refrigerate for at least 2 hours.

4. Transfer the liquid to a punch bowl, top it off with the soda water, and serve. Don't ice the punch; ice the glasses instead.

CHICKEN LIVER PÂTÉ

This is the perfect gateway project for the budding charcuterie maker, ideal for the holiday season when friends and family are constantly in and out of your house and you're looking for something to give them that's a bit more festive than the same old crisps or Doritos. It's quite easy to make, and the result is so luxurious that you'll wish you had discovered it years ago. If you're feeling flush and have the momentum, then substitute half the chicken livers for the same weight in foie gras. Heavenly!

MAKES FOUR 4-OUNCE JARS

1½ ounces ruby port

1½ ounces Madeira

1½ ounces cognac

1 tablespoon finely diced shallot

1 garlic clove

1 bay leaf

1 sprig thyme

9 ounces chicken livers

1 teaspoon kosher salt

1 teaspoon pink curing salt (also called Prague powder #2, or DQ curing salt #2)

½ teaspoon freshly ground black pepper

2 large eggs

1 cup (2 sticks) unsalted butter, diced

3½ tablespoons unsalted butter, melted in the microwave

1. In a medium heavy-bottomed saucepan set over medium heat, combine all the booze plus the shallot, garlic, bay leaf, and thyme and bring it to a simmer. Allow to reduce until syrupy, about 10 minutes. Remove from the heat and let cool.

2. Add the livers, kosher salt, curing salt, and pepper to the wine reduction and place it in a 1-gallon zip-top bag. Crack your eggs into a second zip-top bag and place the diced butter into a third bag.

3. Fill a sink or a very large bowl with very warm water and soak the 3 sealed bags until the butter is melted but not separated. This should take about 15 minutes.

4. Sterilize four 4-ounce mason jars by dunking them in boiling water for 10 minutes; remove them with metal tongs and dry them well. Line a roasting pan with a kitchen towel and place the mason jars on top.

5. Meanwhile, preheat oven to 210°F.

6. Dump the eggs into a blender or food processor and process them for 1 minute. With the blender still running, add the liver mixture and continue blending for 1 to 2 minutes more, until it's silky smooth. With the blender running, slowly add in your liquid butter and process until the butter is fully incorporated. Pass the mousse through a fine-mesh sieve and into a clean bowl.

7. Divide the mixture among the mason jars and cover them individually with plastic wrap. Pour hot tap water into the roasting pan to reach halfway up the jars and bake for 30 to 45 minutes, until they measure 118°F in the center (how's that for precision?). Remove the plastic wrap the second those mousses leave the oven so that water droplets don't have a chance to condense on the surface, and place them in the fridge for about an hour to cool.

8. Top the mousse pots with a layer of melted butter to seal them, then cover with lids and return to the fridge. Allow them 24 hours in the fridge to set up nicely before serving. They will live there quite happily for up to 2 weeks.

A JOINT OF BEEF AND A PROPER GRAVY

I've not lived in England for a very long time, but as the saying goes, you can take the man out of the country, but you'll never take the country out of the man. Roast beef and gravy is what a festive meal in England is all about. When I was the executive chef for the Palihouse Hotel in LA, I used to do a bang-up British roast much like this one that attracted all sorts of famous expats, from football players to actors to musicians, each hungering for a taste of home. It was a blast.

SERVES 6

1 (3- to 4-pound) bone-in rib-eye roast

Kosher salt and freshly ground black pepper

½ cup (1 stick) unsalted butter

1 carrot, chopped

1 onion, chopped

2 ribs celery, chopped

1 leek, chopped and thoroughly washed

1 head garlic, cut in half

½ bottle red wine

2 tablespoons all-purpose flour

5 cups beef stock

1. Hit the rib-eye roast with plenty of salt on all sides, really seasoning the shit out of it. For the best results, do this 24 hours in advance; this helps the seasoning fully penetrate the roast and dries out the surface so that it sears better.

2. Preheat the oven to 325°F.

3. Heat a large roasting pan or Dutch oven on the stovetop over medium heat and add the butter. Allow it to melt and go nut brown and foamy. Place the beef in the pan fat-side down and let it sear for 5 to 7 minutes, until golden brown (always start with the fat cap down, as you want to render away that fat and utilize it for searing the rest of the meat). Repeat the searing on all the sides of the beef. Transfer the beef to a plate and set it aside.

4. Add the carrot, onion, celery, and leek to the pan and sweat them down in the fat for 3 minutes, or until the onions are translucent. Mound up the veggies and garlic and put the beef back on top. Chuck it in the oven, uncovered, for 15 to 18 minutes per pound—so about 1 hour for a roast of this size. You're looking for an internal temperature of 125°F for medium-rare and 130 to 135°F for medium.

5. While the beef cooks, pour the wine into a medium saucepan over high heat and reduce it down by two thirds, about 15 minutes. Set aside.

6. Remove the beef from the oven, transfer it to a cutting board, and tent it with foil to keep the heat and moisture in. Set your roasting pan on the stovetop over medium heat and stir the flour into the pan drippings. Cook, stirring, for 5 to 7 minutes, until it begins to brown. Whisk in the wine in a slow stream, followed by the beef stock. Bring the liquid to a simmer and cook uncovered for 10 to 15 minutes to reduce the volume slightly.

7. Strain the gravy into a pitcher. Slice the beef, working against the grain, and serve with your favorite vegetables and Yorkshire Puddings (page 168).

POTATO AND TURNIP GRATIN

Potato gratin is a classic dish for good reason; there's little on earth that compares to the trio of potatoes, cream, and cheese. If I'm honest, I started adding in turnips to begin with because one of my sous-chefs over-ordered them and we had loads in the fridge to get rid of. But we stumbled onto something truly wonderful, with the sweetness of the turnips balancing out the saltiness of Parmesan cheese. Now I wouldn't do gratin any other way.

SERVES 6

1 tablespoon unsalted butter

2 medium to large turnips

2 pounds peeled Yukon gold potatoes (about 4 large potatoes)

2 cups heavy cream

2 shallots, finely diced

2½ cups grated Parmesan

1 teaspoon salt

½ teaspoon freshly ground black pepper

1. Preheat the oven to 325°F.

2. Butter the inside of a 10 × 15-inch Pyrex or ceramic baking dish. Slice the turnips razor thin, about ¹⁄₁₆ inch, using a very sharp knife or, ideally, a mandoline slicer (watch your fingers, lads; Christmas is a bad time to head to the hospital). Follow with the potatoes.

3. In a medium bowl, mix the sliced turnips with half of the cream, half of the shallots, 1 cup of the Parmesan, and half of the salt and pepper. Repeat in a second bowl with the potatoes.

4. Now we start layering, which is a bit of a swine, but it's necessary. First lay down a single layer of potatoes, followed by a single layer of turnips, and so on and so forth until you run out of both. Pour any excess cream left in the bowls over the top of the gratin. Sprinkle the remaining ½ cup Parmesan over the top.

5. Chuck the gratin in the oven and bake until fork-tender and golden brown, 30 to 45 minutes. Allow it to cool off for 10 minutes before eating, as it will be incredibly hot and would otherwise burn the shit out of your mouth.

YORKSHIRE PUDDINGS

Sunday in England is a family day. Growing up, we'd watch a football match, do some chores (which, of course, I hated), and then a big cooked lunch usually started around 3 or 4 o'clock. This was the main meal of the day on Sundays and we always sat down to it as a family, sometimes with cousins and aunts and uncles added into the mix. There would be three or four types of vegetables, potatoes, gravy, and a roast of some sort: beef with horseradish cream, chicken with sage and onion stuffing, lamb with mint sauce, or pork with applesauce. And there were always Yorkshire puddings, baked golden and puffy. My mother would have to make extra to fill with lemon curd and vanilla so that we kids could eat them for dessert too.

SERVES 6

3 large organic eggs

½ cup all-purpose flour

Pinch of sea salt

1 cup whole milk

12 tablespoons vegetable oil

1. Whisk the eggs together in a medium bowl until pale and fluffy, about 4 minutes. Add the flour, salt, and milk and whisk again until really well incorporated. Pour the batter into a pitcher and let it sit for 30 minutes before you use it.

2. Preheat the oven to 375°F, preferably on the convection setting if you have it (this circulates the air so that the oven temperature stays even throughout). Place a 12-cup muffin pan in the oven to heat up for 5 minutes. Pour 1 tablespoon oil into each cup, put the pan back into the oven, and heat until the oil is very hot and smoking.

3. Dead gently open the oven door, slide the pan halfway out, and carefully pour the batter into the muffin cups to fill them about halfway. You have to be as quick as you can here, otherwise the oil will cool and the puddings will stick, which is obviously not what you want.

4. Close the oven door and cook the Yorkshire puddings for 15 minutes without opening it. You can peek if you want, but it's better to just be patient. Serve them immediately.

EGGNOG ICE CREAM

This eggnog ice cream is delicious on its own, but especially on top of apple pie.

1 pint cream

1 cup whole milk

Pinch of salt

½ vanilla bean, split open and seeds scraped out

1 cup sugar

9 large egg yolks

½ teaspoon freshly grated nutmeg

6 tablespoons dark rum

1. In a heavy-bottomed saucepan over medium heat, combine the cream, milk, salt, and vanilla and bring the mixture to a boil.

2. Meanwhile, in a stand mixer fitted with the whisk attachment, combine the sugar and egg yolks and whisk at medium-high speed until the mixture triples in volume and turns pale yellow, light, and creamy. With the mixer running on medium speed, slowly add the hot cream mixture and continue to process until the liquid reaches room temperature. Stir in the nutmeg and rum and chill the ice cream base in the refrigerator overnight.

3. Spin the base in an ice cream maker according to the manufacturer's instructions.

APPLE PIE

They say in the States that there's nothing more American than apple pie, but I think you can actually thank Great Britain for that one (you're welcome!). We love our apples in the United Kingdom and have hundreds of different varieties, which give us fantastic ciders, preserves, tarts, and, yes, pies. This simple recipe is incredible with scoop of eggnog ice cream—now there's a flavor you Yanks can take credit for through and through.

SERVES 8

2 cups all-purpose flour

1¼ teaspoons salt

⅔ cup plus 2 tablespoons vegetable shortening

4 to 6 tablespoons cold water

6 cups peeled and sliced Pink Lady or Granny Smith apples

¼ cup brown sugar

½ cup granulated sugar

1 teaspoon ground cinnamon

⅛ teaspoon freshly grated nutmeg

⅛ teaspoon ground allspice

1 tablespoon fresh lemon juice

2 tablespoons cornstarch

1. Combine the flour, 1 teaspoon of the salt, and the shortening in a food processor and pulse to blend them together until you have pea-sized flakes. Slowly add the cold water 1 tablespoon at a time until the dough is moist and begins to pull away slightly from the walls of the food processor.

2. Divide the dough into two equal balls. Lightly flour them and flatten into discs. Wrap each tightly in plastic and refrigerate them for at least 45 minutes and up to 24 hours.

3. Preheat the oven to 425°F.

4. Remove the dough from the fridge and grease a pie pan with a bit of shortening or cooking spray. On a lightly floured work surface, roll out one piece of dough into a round slightly larger than the circumference of the upside-down pie pan. Carefully roll the dough around a floured rolling pin; gently unfurl it across the top of the pie pan. Roll a small dough scrap into a little ball, dust it with flour, and use it to gently press the dough into the pie pan (using your warm fingers will often break the dough).

5. In a large bowl, combine the apples, brown sugar, granulated sugar, spices, lemon juice, cornstarch, and remaining ¼ teaspoon salt and mix them well. Scrape them into the pie pan.

6. On a lightly floured work surface, roll out your second piece of dough. Carefully roll the dough around a floured rolling pin; gently unfurl it across the top of the pie pan. Crimp the edges of the crust together with your fingers or a fork to seal the shell. Remove any excess dough with a sharp knife and cut a couple of slits in the center for steam to escape. Place the pie on a baking sheet.

7. Bake the pie for 40 to 50 minutes, until deep golden brown. If you'd like, halfway through baking you can brush the top of the pie with a bit of simple syrup and sprinkle it with large grains of sugar in the raw. Remove the pie from the oven and let it set for at least 2 hours before serving.

PUDDING

IF YOU'RE SCRATCHING YOUR HEAD AND WONDERING WHY I'VE DEVOTED AN ENTIRE chapter to puddings, you can relax: in England, we refer to the entire category of dessert as "pudding." Cakes, tarts, pies, ice cream, cookies, crumbles, cobblers. Puddings, all.

I have a real fondness for baking, more so I think than the average chef. I like the creative aspect of pastry work and the chemistry at play in baking. It's much more technical than savory cooking and tends to require more precision. I might have become a pastry chef, only my hands are always too hot! Which is a disaster when you're working with delicate doughs all day long.

My taste in dessert runs toward the traditional. I'm not a big fan of savory flavors or complicated presentations. I think that a good meal should end with something sweet and comforting. What follows are my most tried-and-true recipes for pudding.

STICKY TOFFEE PUDDING

We English have a horrific sweet tooth, and sate it with all manner of rich, sugary cakes, trifles, and soft, gooey puddings (as well as awesome candy bars, by the way—I have yet to find anything in America that rivals a Cadbury Flake). Sticky toffee pudding is one of our best, and probably the most famous outside England. I have made this recipe more times than I can count and number it among my favorites.

There's not much to it, besides to mix the batter as little as possible. The more air you whisk into the eggs and baking powder, the more the mixture will rise in the oven, and a pudding like this one is meant to be dense enough to put you into a good food coma for two to three hours.

SERVES 4

2 cups heavy cream

½ cup dark brown sugar

2½ teaspoons Tate & Lyle's Golden Syrup or molasses

Fine sea salt

8 to 10 pitted Medjool dates

1 cup water

1 teaspoon baking soda

1⅓ cups all-purpose flour

1 teaspoon baking powder

4 tablespoons (½ stick) unsalted butter

¾ cup granulated sugar

4 large eggs

1 teaspoon vanilla extract

1 tablespoon brewed espresso

1 teaspoon black treacle (aka blackstrap molasses)

Whipped cream, ice cream, or crème fraîche for serving

1. Preheat the oven to 350°F and butter an 8½-inch porcelain soufflé dish (or a baking dish of a similar size).

2. Knock together the toffee sauce by bringing the cream, brown sugar, golden syrup, and a pinch of salt to a boil in a medium saucepan over medium-high heat, stirring often to melt the sugar. Lower the heat and simmer, stirring constantly, for about 5 minutes, until the mixture is thick and coats the back of your spoon. Pour half of the sauce into the prepared soufflé dish and place the dish in the freezer. Set aside the other half.

3. Now to the pudding. Heat the dates and water in a medium saucepan set over medium-high heat. Once the water begins to boil, remove the pan from the heat and stir in the baking soda. Set the pan aside someplace where you can keep it slightly warm.

4. Grab a medium bowl and sift together the flour, baking powder, and ½ teaspoon salt.

5. In the bowl of a stand mixer fitted with the paddle attachment (hopefully—or you can do this by hand), beat the butter and granulated sugar until light and fluffy. Gradually beat in the eggs, then the vanilla, followed by the espresso and black treacle. It's going to look sort of curdled, but that's normal. Stir in half of the flour mixture, then the dates and water, then add the remaining flour mixture until just barely mixed. Don't overbeat the batter, or when you cook it, it will raise up like a fifteenth-century Scottish rebel group.

6. Remove the soufflé dish from the freezer and scrape in the batter. Bake for 50 minutes, or until a toothpick inserted into the center of the pudding comes out with moist crumbs attached.

7. Spoon portions of the cake into serving bowls and douse it with your reserved warm toffee sauce. Serve with whipped cream, ice cream, or crème fraîche—whatever takes your fancy.

CHOCOLATE MARQUISE WITH CARAMELIZED BANANAS

English people take their chocolate very seriously. I absolutely love Cadbury brand, which is nothing fancy but truly delicious. Ever since I was a kid I could eat unhealthy amounts in a single sitting. I have to admit that Cadbury is better suited to eating than cooking, though—for cooking, I use either Valrhona or Cacao Barry brands in my restaurant, and these are the chocolates I would recommend to you.

Another particular sweet tooth addiction for me is bananas, one of Mother Nature's ready-made desserts. I have fond memories of going to the Mansfield open market with my mum and hearing the local green grocer shouting out his bounty ("Come get your bananas, 25 p a pound! Come on, love, you know you want a banana . . .").

For me, it makes complete sense to bring together two of my favorite ingredients in one dessert. Have your insulin ready for the glycerin shock that's about to hit you, because it is seriously sweet and rich!

SERVES 6 TO 8

1 (14-ounce) can sweetened condensed milk

1 pound high-quality milk chocolate, chopped

4 tablespoons (½ stick) unsalted butter, cut into pieces

1 cup cold heavy cream

1 cup sugar

½ vanilla bean

2 to 3 bananas

1 pint chocolate chip or dulce de leche ice cream, optional

1. Make the dulce de leche: Bring a medium pot of water to a boil and insert the sealed can of condensed milk. Let it boil for 4 hours, making sure to top off the water whenever necessary so that the pan doesn't boil dry (alternately, 45 minutes in a pressure cooker will do the job). Remove the can from the heat and let it cool before opening; inside, the milk should be thick and caramel colored.

2. Lightly oil a 6-cup loaf pan (about 8½ × 4 inches in dimension), line it with plastic wrap, and set it aside.

3. In the top of a double boiler or in a metal bowl set over a pan of simmering water, combine the chocolate and butter and melt until smooth, stirring occasionally. Remove from the heat and allow to cool.

4. In the bowl of a stand mixer fitted with the whisk attachment, beat the cream with 2 tablespoons of the dulce de leche and ½ cup of the sugar. Slit open the vanilla bean and scrape the seeds into the mixture. Whip on medium speed until stiff peaks form. Whisk about one third of the cream into the cooled chocolate, then gently fold in the remaining whipped cream. Pour the chocolate mixture into the prepared pan, smoothing the top with a rubber spatula. Cover with plastic wrap and chill it overnight.

5. Unwrap the marquise, invert it onto a platter, and shake gently to release. Remove the plastic wrap from the top and let sit at room temperature for about 15 minutes to soften.

6. Meanwhile, peel and cut the bananas lengthwise and sprinkle the remaining ½ cup sugar liberally but evenly along the flat side of each banana half. Using a butane kitchen torch, flame the bananas until golden and caramelized (the dish is sweet, so a bit of burnt sugar won't hurt—if you go a fraction *Pulp Fiction* on it, don't worry, it'll still be delicious). If you don't have a torch, you can also pop the bananas under a broiler set on high.

7. Slice the marquise into ¾- to 1-inch-thick pieces and divide them among dessert plates. Top each slice with a piece of banana and a scoop of ice cream, if you wish, then drizzle the whole thing with dulce de leche sauce.

DULCE DE LECHE SAUCE

MAKES 1½ CUPS

1 cup heavy cream
**4 heaping tablespoons
Dulce de Leche (page 176)**
2 teaspoons rum

In the bowl of a stand mixer fitted with a whisk attachment, gently whip together the cream, dulce de leche, and rum until the mixture begins to thicken and coats the back of a spoon. Refrigerate until ready to use.

LEMON TART

My grandma is not a great cook. She's almost one hundred years old as I write this recipe, which means she was born bang in the middle of World War I and was just entering adulthood during World War II—no time to worry about kitchen skills with a war effort on! She was always a career woman, working into her seventies and only taking time off to have her three children. But she did know how to bake a little bit, and would make cakes and biscuits, my favorite jam, and lemon tarts.

Now before anyone gets excited that this recipe might be a family heirloom, it most certainly is not. Grandma's was made using store-bought lemon curd and a dough made from lard. It did, however, give me an early appreciation for the dessert, so when I moved to the big smoke (aka London) I genuinely thought I was a lemon curd expert. Then I ate a lemon tart at Marco Pierre White's Criterion Brasserie, and it was one of those moments in life when you realize you don't know shit and you have to start at square one.

This isn't Marco's recipe either; his takes incredible skill to cook correctly. But this is a very good lemon tart, in some respects equal to his, just a lot easier for the home cook to master.

SERVES 8

¾ cup (1½ sticks) cold unsalted butter

2 cups sugar

½ teaspoon pure vanilla extract

1¾ cups all-purpose flour

¼ teaspoon salt

2 cups rice or pie weights

4 lemons, at room temperature

½ cup (1 stick) unsalted butter, at room temperature

4 extra-large eggs, at room temperature

1. In the bowl of a stand mixer fitted with the paddle attachment, mix together the cold butter with ½ cup of the sugar until they are just combined. Add the vanilla.

2. In a medium bowl, sift together the flour and ⅛ teaspoon of the salt, then add to the butter and sugar mixture. Mix on low speed just until the dough comes together. Dump it out onto a flour-dusted surface and shape the dough into a flat disk. Wrap it in plastic wrap and refrigerate for 20 minutes.

3. On a flour-dusted work surface, roll the dough into an 11-inch round. Curl it around your rolling pin and unfurl it on top of a removable-bottom tart pan 10 inches in diameter. With cold hands so as not to melt the butter, gently press the dough into the pan, slicing any excess off the edges. Chuck the tart shell back in the fridge for 20 minutes to rest; this keeps it from shrinking when baked.

4. Preheat the oven to 350°F.

5. Lay 4 sheets of plastic wrap over the top of the tart shell and fill it with the rice or pie weights. Bake for 20 to 25 minutes, until the dough begins to lightly brown. Lift out the weights and bake for 20 to 25 minutes more, until golden brown. Remove the tart shell from the oven and leave it on the counter to cool.

6. Using a Microplane, zest the lemons into a small bowl, being careful to avoid the white pith. Squeeze the lemons to yield ½ cup juice.

7. In the bowl of a stand mixer fitted with the paddle attachment, cream the room-temperature butter, the remaining 1½ cups sugar, and the lemon zest

(continued)

until pale and fluffy; this will take 5 to 6 minutes, scraping the bowl down with a spatula from time to time.

8. Add the eggs one at a time, then add the lemon juice and the remaining ⅛ teaspoon salt. Mix until combined.

9. Pour the lemon curd into a 2-quart saucepan and cook it over low heat, stirring constantly with a rubber spatula, until thickened, about 10 minutes (the lemon curd will thicken when it reaches about 175°F, or just below a simmer). Remove it from the heat.

10. Fill the tart shell with warm lemon curd and allow it to set at room temperature. Once cooled to room temperature, the tart can be chilled in the refrigerator.

CREPES SUZETTE

With the way that food is going these days, it seems like everyone is outmaneuvering each other to come up with the edgiest and most original dessert. Me? I like my sweets classic and delicious—full stop. Crepes Suzette is an example of an elegant French recipe that has stood the test of time. When I was young and before my parents decided they didn't like each other anymore, my family did a very typical English thing and stuffed ourselves into a caravan like sardines and drove to France. It's not a great way to travel (come to think of it, maybe that's why they didn't like each other so much!), but once we got there it was brilliant. La Rochelle, a beautiful town in the south of France, was our usual destination. These trips were my first experience eating proper crepes, and they taught me how you can make the most extraordinary and unforgettable food using just a few simple flavors.

Assuming you don't have a crepe pan (and honestly, your average household does not need a crepe pan), go with something made from Teflon. There is absolutely no margin of error when cooking paper-thin crepes, so you need a surface that's entirely nonstick.

SERVES 4 TO 6

1 cup all-purpose flour

½ cup whole milk

½ cup less
1 tablespoon water

2 large eggs

About 1 pound (4 sticks)
unsalted butter

¼ cup sugar

1½ teaspoons orange zest

½ cup freshly squeezed
orange juice

4 ounces Grand Marnier

¼ teaspoon salt

1 pint vanilla ice cream

Segments from
4 to 6 oranges

1. Whisk together the flour, milk, water, eggs, and 2 tablespoons melted butter until you have a completely smooth batter. Now stick it in the fridge to rest for at least 20 minutes or up to 24 hours (the longer, the better).

2. Melt about 1 tablespoon butter in a crepe pan or 9-inch Teflon skillet over medium-low heat. Add 3 tablespoons of batter to the pan and swirl until the bottom of the pan is covered with batter. Cook the crepe for 1 minute, or until slightly moist on top and golden underneath.

3. Loosen the edges of the crepe, slide the spatula under it, then gently flip it upside down in the pan. Cook for 1 minute and transfer the crepe to a plate to keep warm. Repeat the process with the remaining batter, buttering the pan again before each addition.

4. Melt 2 sticks of butter in a large skillet over medium heat. Stir in the sugar, orange zest, orange juice, Grand Marnier, and salt. Let it continue to bubble until the sauce thickens and the bubbles begin to slow, about 5 minutes. Dip a spoon into the sauce and run your finger across the back; if your finger leaves a trail through the sauce, it's ready.

5. Very delicately lay a crepe flat in the pan, coating one side with sauce. Fold it in quarters and transfer it to a plate. Repeat with the remaining crepes, arranging them 3 per plate. Add a scoop of ice cream and a drizzle of extra sauce over the top. Garnish with orange segments.

BRIOCHE DOUGHNUTS WITH BOURBON GLAZE

In my first couple of years out of culinary school, I worked as a commis at Café Royal on Piccadilly Circus, just as a Dunkin' Donuts was going in a few doors down. I had never had a doughnut before—they are very much an American import—but I quickly learned that doughnuts are something of a perfect food when you are young, broke, and working weird hours. I liked them so much that I set to work designing a version that would fit into a restaurant context. This recipe was on the menu at Waterloo & City for most of the time that restaurant was in business due to its tremendous appeal with our diners. It is seriously decadent. Brioche is buttery and rich to begin with, before you go dunking it in hot oil and finishing it with a buttery bourbon glaze.

MAKES 12 TO 18

⅔ cup cold whole milk

2 tablespoons dry active yeast

3½ cups all-purpose flour

¼ cup sugar

2 teaspoons salt

2 large cold eggs

5 large cold egg yolks

1¼ cups (2½ sticks) cold butter, cubed

Cooking oil

Bourbon Glaze (recipe follows)

1. Place half of the milk in a small bowl and warm it in the microwave until lukewarm. Stir in the yeast and leave it for 3 to 4 minutes to dissolve.

2. In the bowl of a stand mixer fitted with a paddle attachment, mix the flour, sugar, and salt well. Slowly add the eggs and yolks, then scrape the bowl down. Add the remaining (cold) milk and mix well. Add the yeast mixture.

3. With the mixer on medium-high speed, slowly add the butter a few cubes at a time, allowing it to become mostly incorporated before adding more.

4. Line a baking sheet with parchment paper and spray it with cooking spray. Transfer the dough to the prepared sheet, cover it with plastic wrap, and let it rest in the fridge overnight.

5. On a floured work surface, roll out the dough to about ½-inch thick. Using a floured biscuit cutter, cut the dough into rounds 1 to 1½ inches in diameter. Let the doughnuts sit in a warm room until doubled in size, 8 to 10 minutes.

6. If you've got an electric fryer by chance, use it, because they're way safer; if not, take a heavy pot like a Dutch oven and fill it two thirds full with cooking oil. Position a thermometer in the oil and heat it nice and slow over medium heat until the temperature reads 350°F. Working a few at a time (don't crowd the pot, gents), fry the doughnuts until golden brown, about 2 minutes per side. Remove from the fryer with a slotted spoon to a paper towel-lined baking sheet. Toss each doughnut in bourbon glaze while still warm, or serve the glaze on the side. Eat immediately.

BOURBON GLAZE

MAKES 2½ CUPS

1 cup dark brown sugar

Seeds from ¼ vanilla bean

1½ teaspoons light corn syrup

1 cup sweetened condensed milk

½ cup (1 stick) unsalted butter, diced

1 tablespoon bourbon

1. In a medium saucepan over medium-high heat, combine the brown sugar, vanilla bean, and corn syrup and bring the mixture to a boil, whisking constantly.

2. Once the brown sugar is fully melted, reduce the mixture to a simmer and add the condensed milk, butter, and bourbon. Continue to simmer, stirring, until all the butter is incorporated and the glaze is smooth.

ETON MESS

For a small island, England has always had plenty of social divides: upper class vs. working class, northerners vs. southerners, East Enders vs. Coronation Street (the country's two favorite soaps), your football team vs. his football team, you name it and the English will bicker over it.

This lovely dessert of strawberries, cream, and meringue is known in the south of England (and now, around the world) as Eton Mess, named after a very posh school that Prince William attended. Up north where I come from, we just call it strawberries, cream, and meringue, because we're not posh and weren't born toffee-nosed with silver spoons wedged up our arses!

Whatever you call it, it is an absolute stunner when the strawberries are fresh and local, and relatively easy to put together (you can even use store-bought meringue to speed up the process if you like). As a kid, we used to make this dessert with the wild strawberries growing in my auntie's garden, and it was simply divine.

SERVES 4

1 pound strawberries, topped and coarsely chopped

3 tablespoons granulated sugar

1 cup heavy cream

¼ cup confectioners' sugar

3 cups meringue pieces, smashed up to bite-sized (recipe follows)

1 pint vanilla ice cream

1. Mix together the strawberries and granulated sugar in a large bowl, cover it with plastic wrap, and let it sit for 30 minutes to draw the strawberries' juices out. Strain the strawberries, reserving the juice.

2. Whisk together the cream and confectioners' sugar in a large bowl until soft peaks form. Gently fold the meringue pieces and berries into the whipped cream.

3. Place some of the strawberry, cream, and meringue mixture in the bottom of your bowls. Add a scoop of vanilla ice cream, then top with more mess, drizzle the reserved strawberry juice over the mess for a wonderful sauce, and eat your heart out.

MERINGUE

YIELDS 1 LARGE MERINGUE

3 large egg whites
¼ teaspoon cream of tartar
¾ cup superfine sugar
¼ teaspoon pure vanilla extract

1. Preheat the oven to 200°F. Line a baking sheet with wax paper, and if you've got some, hit it with nonstick cooking spray too just in case.

2. In the bowl of an electric stand mixer fitted with the whisk attachment, beat the egg whites on medium-low speed until foamy. Add the cream of tartar and continue to beat the whites until they hold soft peaks.

3. Add the sugar a little at a time and continue to whisk, on medium-high speed, until the meringue holds very stiff peaks. Add the vanilla. The meringue is done when it holds stiff peaks and when you rub a little between your thumb and index finger it does not feel sandy. If it feels gritty, the sugar has not fully melted, so keep going.

4. Spread the meringue onto your baking sheet about ¾-inch thick and as evenly as possible. Bake for 1½ to 1¾ hours, turning the baking sheet halfway through to make sure it bakes evenly. The meringue is done when it is pure white and fairly crisp.

5. Turn off the oven, open the door a crack, and leave the meringue in the oven to finish drying out for an hour or two (or as long as overnight). Store it in an airtight container.

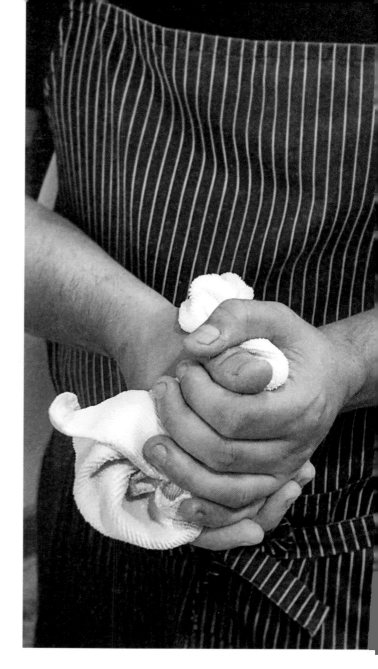

CHOCOLATE AND CARAMEL TRIFLE WITH THE NOSTALGIA OF TWIX

As I've said before, I think the best desserts are the simple and satisfying ones, and a Twix and a glass of milk is one of my all-time favorite vices. Several years back I got to thinking about how I could combine those fabulous flavors of chocolate, caramel, and cookie into a more modern, restaurant-ready dessert. I knew right off the bat that I would do the chocolate component in silky, smooth panna cotta form, and shortbread was the obvious stand-in for Twix's crispy biscuit base. But straight caramel would turn out way too sickly sweet in the kind of portion size we were looking at doing. Since Twix and a glass of milk make such a good pairing, I thought why not work the milk right into the dessert with a creamy dulce de leche caramel? And there you have it: my take on Twix.

SERVES 8

SHORTBREAD
2 cups (4 sticks)
unsalted butter

1 cup confectioners' sugar

¾ teaspoon salt

Seeds from 1 vanilla bean

3 ¾ cups all-purpose flour

DULCE DE LECHE CREAM
1⅛ teaspoons
powdered gelatin

10 large egg yolks

2 (8-ounce) jars dulce
de leche (see note)

10 large egg whites

CHOCOLATE PANNA COTTA
2½ teaspoons gelatin

2 cups heavy cream

2 cups whole milk

½ cup sugar

8 ounces dark chocolate

1. Make the shortbread: In a stand mixer fitted with a paddle attachment, cream together the butter, confectioners' sugar, salt, and vanilla seeds. Add the flour and mix until just incorporated.

2. Flatten the dough into a disc, wrap it in plastic wrap, and refrigerate it for at least 1 hour or up to 24 hours.

3. Preheat the oven to 350°F.

4. On a floured work surface, roll out the shortbread to about ¼ inch thick. Transfer it to a baking sheet lined with parchment paper and bake until golden brown, 10 to 12 minutes. Set aside.

5. Make the dulce de leche cream: In a small bowl, sprinkle the gelatin over 2 tablespoons of room temperature water. Set it aside to bloom while you work.

6. In a stand mixer fitted with the whisk attachment, whip together the egg yolks and three quarters of the dulce de leche until the mixture doubles in volume, 5 to 7 minutes. Scrape it into a large bowl and set aside.

7. Beat the egg whites in the mixer in a clean bowl until they form stiffish peaks. Scrape them into a separate bowl and set them aside.

8. In a small saucepan set over medium heat, warm the remaining dulce de leche until not quite simmering. Whisk in the gelatin. Remove the mixture from the heat and slowly whisk it into the egg yolk mixture; be careful not to combine the two too quickly, or the heat will cause the yolks to curdle and you'll have a proper mess on your hands. Fold in the egg whites and set aside.

9. Make the chocolate panna cotta: In a small bowl, sprinkle the gelatin over ¼ cup pf room temperature water. Set it aside to bloom while you work.

10. In a medium saucepan set over medium-high heat, combine the cream, milk, and sugar and bring to a boil. Break the chocolate into small chunks and place it in a large bowl.

11. Pour the boiling cream over the top and let it sit for a minute or two to melt the chocolate. Whisk until completely incorporated and let it cool slightly. Whisk in the gelatin. Let cool to room temperature, then refrigerate until set, about 1½ hours in total.

12. To build the dessert: Break the shortbread into even-sized chunks, reserving the shortbread crumbs, and use half of them to line the bottom of an 8 × 10 × 2-inch Pyrex dish in an even layer. Cover that with the dulce de leche cream. Repeat with another layer of shortbread and refrigerate for at least 1 hour. Top with the chocolate panna cotta, then sprinkle the top with your shortbread crumbs. Allow to set in the refrigerator overnight.

Note: If you fancy making your own Dulce de Leche, see page 176 for instructions.

INDEX

THANK YOU

- to Kyle Cathie for trusting in me and helping me publish this book

- to Liz Gunnison Dunn for putting up with my busy schedule while writing this book

- to Jessica Goodman, my editor, who occasionally had to jump up and down to get my attention, but it was all worth it

- to everybody who took part in creating this book, including Sharon Bowers, Joh Morris, Judith Hannam, Claire Rogers, Jean Cazals, Alison Lew, Curtis Stone, and Jon Taffer

- to Sybil and Harry, my grandparents, for putting me through cooking school

- to Eden and Saffy who stand with me through thick and thin

- to all the employees who worked for me and put up with my bullshit

This book is dedicated to Saffron Rose Collins, who makes everything better. Love, Daddy

Published in 2015 by Kyle Books
www.kylebooks.com

Distributed by National Book Network
4501 Forbes Blvd, Suite 200, Lanham, MD 20706
Phone: (800) 462-6420   Fax: (800) 338-4550
customercare@nbnbooks.com

10 9 8 7 6 5 4 3 2 1

ISBN 978-1-909487-33-8

Text © 2016 Brendan Collins
Design © 2016 Kyle Books
Photographs © 2016 Jean Cazals

Brendan Collins is hereby identified as the author of this work in accordance with Section 77 of the Copyright, Designs and Patents Act 1988.

Project Editor: Jessica Goodman
Copy Editor: Leda Scheintaub
Designer: Alison Lew, Vertigo Design NYC
Photographer: Jean Cazals
Food Stylist: Marie-Ange Lapierre
Prop Stylist: Tamzin Ferdinando
Production: Nic Jones, Gemma John, and Lisa Pinnell

Library of Congress Control Number: 2015953140

Color reproduction by ALTA London
Printed and bound in China by 1010 International Printing Ltd.